*The Fragility
of Knowledge*

The Fragility of Knowledge

Theological Education in the Church and the University

EDWARD FARLEY

FORTRESS PRESS   PHILADELPHIA

Copyright © 1988 by Fortress Press

Library of Congress Cataloging-in-Publication Data

Farley, Edward, 1929–
    The fragility of knowledge.

    Continues: Theologia.
    1. Theology—Study and teaching. I. Title.
BV4020.F348 1988   230'.07   86-46438
ISBN 0-8006-2080-1

2991K87   Printed in the United States of America   1–2080

Dedicated to
Robert Wood Lynn

Contents

Preface

This volume of essays constitutes a sequel to *Theologia: The Fragmentation and Unity of Theological Education*, which appeared several years ago. *Theologia*, in undertaking an "archaeological" history of clergy education, interrogated and criticized current North American Protestant clergy education by retrieving an older understanding of theology. The work, however, had its limitations: it restricted its attention to clergy education and thus neglected whole provinces of possible theological education; it failed to explore alternatives to professionalist paradigms; and it shrank from offering positive proposals about the structure of theological study. These essays take up the issues that were slighted in the earlier work. Though the essays build on that work, they can be read by themselves. Only four of the eight essays were written in independent settings, and all eight come together, I think, into a coherent line of argument. A brief account of this argument may help the reader situate the essays in relationship to one another.

Theologia contended that "theology" in its primary sense refers to the reflective wisdom of the believer and that scholarship (science) and education describe theology in a valid but secondary and derived sense. Cut loose from theology's primary sense, clergy education is really less an education in *theology* than the facilitation of clerical skills. As such the movement of its studies is from relatively autonomous and isolated "theoretical" studies in Bible, history, ethics, and systematics to practical or facilitative studies. The essays of this volume supplement and refine the description of theology as the reflective wisdom of the believer. Theological reflection is constituted by fundamental modes of interpretation that focus on different aspects of the believer's situation. The reflective life of the believer is, in other words, a hermeneutic orientation, not in the narrow sense of interpreting texts but in the broader sense of interpreting whatever presents itself for response and understanding.

These essays, then, begin where *Theologia* left off. On the basis of this hermeneutic approach they explore theology and theological education in the settings of university education, clergy education, and church education. If theology is part of the interpreting life of the believer as such, then its study is a responsibility not just of clergy education but of church education (chap. 5). If it is legitimate and important for the university to study *religion* and specific *religions*, the university cannot restrict its study to the exposition of phenomenal data, thereby ignoring the claims the religions embody. It is true that university studies of religions do not have their rationale in the needs of believers or communities of faith, but they are obligated to take seriously and to study the basic modes of self-interpretation of the religions. That is why the university study of the Christian religion will reproduce in some way the structure of theological study (chap. 4). This line of argument occurs at the end of a more general analysis of the current situation of the university, a situation brought about in part by the repression of the hermeneutical complexity of the Enlightenment tradition (chaps. 1 and 2). This repression can be attributed to a new social entity that functions as the vehicle for both research and pedagogy: the specialty field (chap. 3).

When theology in the sense of reflective interpretation is disciplined by cognitively oriented inquiry in an educational setting, we have the *study of theology,* and this study is shaped by both its subject matter, the Christian faith, and its aims, the disciplining of the modes of interpretation intrinsic to the situation of faith. The structure of theological study which results will be appropriate to all the settings of the study of theology—those of university education, clergy education, and church education alike (chaps. 7 and 8). Postbaccalaureate clergy education as a specific instance of theological study requires the full appropriation of scholarship because of the level of its study of both the subject matter and the modes of interpretation (chap. 6).

Such is the line of argument. Its unity is a hermeneutic approach to theological study. I use the term "hermeneutic" with some misgivings. Hermeneutic can be written off as the latest fad of academic theologians. Furthermore, it sometimes has the rather narrow connotation of a science of texts and of methods of dealing with texts. In spite of these disadvantages, I stay with the term. Hermeneutic correlates closely with the notion of understanding and, in a broadened sense, refers to the acts of interpretation that yield understanding. Thus, "hermeneutic modes" means "modes of interpretation." Hermeneutic can also be used in a meta- sense, for the inquiry into what interpretation is and what properly governs it. "Interpretation" and "understanding" better express what human beings do when they reflectively and assessively respond to situations than the language of technical cognitive inquiry—"knowledge," "certainty," and "demonstration." At the same time these terms better express the cognitive aspect of the human response to situations than terms like "experience," "insight," "intuition," or "perception."

The three chapters on the structure of theological study (chaps. 6–8) are the culmination of this work, toward which the other chapters build. The supporting chapters explore several settings of theological study. The material on the university and on lay education in the church is idealizing and futuristic, because the study of theology has not yet taken hold in these settings. Because religious studies in the university and lay education in the church are not yet pursued in close relation to theological study, the university and church are discussed as settings of future theological study. Clergy education continues to be the primary seat of theological studies; hence specific criticisms and curricular suggestions are pointed more directly to it than to the other two settings.

A word is called for about the idiosyncrasies of this collection. A frequent demur occurs in the essays: the structures and patterns I propose do not determine an ideal *curriculum*. A curriculum is a pattern of a specific school in a specific context, and it can never be prescribed in general. Hence, the book consciously forgoes specific curricular proposals. The line of argument of the collection develops through a conceptual apparatus and a use of terms that sometimes depart from common parlance. Some older terms are given restricted meanings to which the reader needs to be alert—for instance, the terms "science" and "discipline." In some cases new terms are offered to designate new phenomena—for example, "specialty fields," "hermeneutic of situations," "modes of interpretation." Or they are offered to avoid the unhappy connotations of the standard terms—for example, "clergy education," "ordered learning." I have retained the term but expanded the meaning of "practical theology." "Believer" occurs frequently, and means simply an active participant in a community of faith. I tend to use Schleiermacher's term "church leadership" instead of "ministry," because of recent broadenings of the latter term. Because I see theological education as possible and desirable in contexts beyond clergy schools—in the university and in the church—I usually use the term "clergy education" to refer to postbaccalaureate seminary and divinity-school courses of study. Because "education" has undergone such an expansion of meaning, referring in some circles to any and all ways an environment forms its participants, I have substituted the term "ordered learning" for "education" when a cumulative, cognitively oriented, and rigorizing course of study is in view. Some of the essays, especially those on the structure of theological study, are written in a denser style than I would like. I regret this and appeal for the reader's patience. To use concepts and paradigms in vogue would have been even more obscuring than to use the concepts I have developed to untangle the problems.

Works of this sort always need the stimulation and reaction of many individuals and social environments. In a few cases the essays were responses to specific invitations, for which I can only be grateful. Craig Dykstra, editing a special issue of *Theology Today* on church education, invited me to contribute to that collection. Stan Lusby, Linda Tober, and others involved in a study of theology and religious studies in the Southeast which was sponsored by the Lilly Endowment invited me to contribute an essay to that venture. The first two essays in the book served as the Mendenhall Lectures at DePauw University in the fall of 1985. Dean Jack Forstman, Walter Harrelson, and John Compton, of Vanderbilt University, and Jack Seymour, of Scarritt College, responded to my need for critical assessment of these essays; Barbara Wheeler, my co-worker on this project, gave exceedingly close critical attention to the essays. Finally, there is no way a few words can do justice to the role Robert Lynn has played in evoking this and other studies of education in the university, the seminary, and the church. He has been and continues to be the shaker and mover of theological education. What is more, he shakes and moves through intellectual curiosity, ongoing study, and a passion for reform; and for this, I—and I am sure, others—express gratitude.

PART 1

THEOLOGY AND
UNIVERSITY EDUCATION

1

The Fragility of Knowledge: Hermeneutic Paradigms in the Enlightenment Tradition

The idea of a university combines the undertaking of inquiry and discovery with educational process, of teaching with scholarly work. Knowledge, therefore, is the university's business, its remuneration and responsibility. Nowadays, many in the university experience themselves living in a besieged community, a cognitive ghetto in a society increasingly alienated from the riches of past learning and from the present resources of genuine culture. It is tempting to view the university as an island of knowledge encircled by hungry anti-intellectual sharks. What prompts suspicion about the idealizing picture of the university in service of pure truth, however, is the very fragility of knowledge. Knowledge is the experience of being laid hold of by evidencing realities. But knowledge, like all human acts and achievements, is part of the flow of history, nature, and the experiencing self. It is not, then, the stamp of a timeless content on the mind but an ongoing individual and social struggle that occurs within agreed-upon paradigms, weighted perspectives, institutional agendas, and heavily nuanced and even infected discourses. Knowledge, therefore, is fragile, since it is more a responsive activity than a precious possession, a "torch of smoky pine that lights the pathway but one step across a void of mystery," to quote Santayana. Fragile knowledge is also corruptible. Its wares are available to the children of darkness.

The modern university is an accumulation of certain landmark periods of the past. Ghosts of Greece and Rome, the medieval monasteries, the European Renaissance linger in its corridors. Few will doubt that the decisive shaper of the modern university is the European Enlightenment. The university's present ethos is in large part determined

3

by the way that it has or has not retained the Enlightenment and the correctives subsequent to the Enlightenment. I shall try, then, to explore the fragility of the university's knowledge by looking at these ancestors, using what Michel Foucault, following Nietzsche, called genealogical method. The ancestors include some that the university has tried to forget, and there are even some skeletons in its closet it would try to hide. I should say at the outset that I am using the term "university" as a shorthand word for all institutions of higher education: colleges, liberal arts programs, professional schools, graduate schools.

Critical Knowledge:
The Enlightenment Ideal

The Enlightenment encompasses an epoch of European culture, a broad cultural ethos, and an ideal. The age was roughly the eighteenth century. The ethos occurred in circles of high culture and learning and was borne by intellectuals, scientists, educators, and scholars of Europe: Diderot and Voltaire, Francis Bacon and Isaac Newton, Goethe and Kant. The ideal was a vision of a society progressing toward harmony and justice under the guidance of leaders unhampered by superstition, prejudice, or authority, and willing to allow pure reason to be their guide.

This Enlightenment ideal is not just a commitment to knowledge. The commitment to knowledge is found in ancient Hellenism, the so-called Middle Ages, and the Renaissance. The Enlightenment's commitment to knowledge begins with a fundamental intuition into the historicity and relativity of all human accomplishments. These include the accomplishments of reason itself, all of which must be assessed and reassessed. This means that knowledge is culturally embodied. It is shaped by the world views and social agendas of the society in which it occurs. It is carried by words and writings that are laden with ambiguity, interpretation, and errancy. The words that knowledge employs are never mere obedient emissaries of reality. The result is that human knowledge is never an absolutely settled accomplishment. As historical it is always a candidate for further inquiry, renewed clarification, new discursive forms. In other words, the accomplishment of knowledge always occurs as criticism. Present knowledge occurs in continued and relentless criticism of past knowledge, a pressing for the establishment of the basis, evidence, and assumptions of any claim. The Enlightenment ideal is, therefore, the ideal of critically accomplished knowledge. And this is why the Enlightenment contrasted itself to the dogmatic temper, to knowledge by tutelage, to mere appeals to the authoritative past. Under the ruthless instrument of criticism (the Enlightenment called it reason), there were no exceptions. Not a single one of the stunning cognitive successes of the past could be taken for granted, not the great founders of Western philosophy, not the architectonic vision of the thirteenth century, not even the highest claim of all, the claim of the church that its truths came from God. In Diderot's words, "Everything must be examined, without exception and without circumspection." This principle does not mean that everything is now discredited. The principle does not counsel mere negation or cynicism. Nor need it represent an undue trust in what critical reason can do. But it does repudiate all professed infallibilities, all asserted inerrancies, that deny their own historical character. This is the university's heritage, and when the university enters onto the tasks of knowledge, it pursues the critically determined knowledge that was the Enlightenment ideal.

Corrected Knowledge:
The Enlightenment Tradition

The first thing that will occur to anyone who hears these words is that the Enlightenment ideal, the critical principle, is itself historical. It too has a historical origin, is heavily nuanced in language, occurs in different interpretations. We must distinguish between the Enlightenment ideal as a formal principle, the principle of unqualified critical assessment and inquiry, and the various historical embodiments of the ideal, including that of the Enlightenment itself. For the Enlightenment promoted not simply reason but a certain understanding of reason. Its corrective was directed not only at the prejudicial temper that would stifle inquiry but at a certain way of construing reason itself. The Enlightenment age moved toward what Francis Bacon called a new organon, a new instrument of knowledge. New as opposed to what? Prior to the Enlightenment what did it mean to be a scientist, a scholar, a member of the community of learning? Two things dominated the pre-Enlightenment road to knowledge: classical languages, which opened up the texts of the past, and logic, the instrument or organon of demonstration. With the Enlightenment came a new primacy and a new instrument: the primacy of experienced data, and the instrument of empirical inquiry. This "logic of facts," as Ernst Cassirer calls it, was not simply a naive rationalism but an empiricism that eventually penetrated most of the university disciplines from the so-called hard sciences to the social sciences and even humanities. The Enlightenment, therefore, is still very much with us, both in its ideal of critically acquired knowledge and in its empiricist paradigm for the operation of criticism.

According to the critical principle, no human interpretation, not even reason's own interpretation of itself, is beyond criticism. Such was the power of the critical principle that subsequent movements reacted critically to the Enlightenment's own account of reason. Three of these movements constitute major criticisms, or better, correctives, of the Enlightenment: the romantic, the theological, and the political. The code words of these correctives are "intuitive imagination," "tradition," and "praxis."

It might be wiser on my part not to use the name "romanticism" for the first corrective. Some see romanticism as a shallow sentimentalism and cult of feeling, now discredited and surpassed by whatever it is our present age is up to. Even such a scholar as Irving Babbitt reduces it to the primitivism of Jean Jacques Rousseau. Such caricatures of the romantic movement miss the heart of the matter, the recovery and formulation of the intuitive imagination. Like the other two correctives, the romantic corrective embodies a certain insight. It constitutes a truth about things. How could anything critical of the "logic of facts" be true? When we do begin with the facts, how do we make cognitive headway? The empiricist tradition soon found out, and the result was the astonishing scientific and engineering successes that produced the modern world. The way one obtains empirical knowledge is, paradoxically, to suspend the immediacy and concreteness of the experienced entity so as to focus very precisely on one of its selected, researchable aspects—for instance, on how certain alloys behave under highly specified conditions, or on a genetic linkage with a certain enzyme deficiency. Concrete reality occurs in a large system of ever-changing relations and events. A human being is not just its anatomical structure. A city is not simply its population distribution. But to be successful, the logic of facts must focus not on the concrete reality but on the selected problem. In other words it must perpetrate an abstraction for the sake of rigor, evidence, and precision. It must violate the concrete reality in order to understand it, or as the saying goes, kill the patient in order to save it.

It is just this abstracting that was the target of the romantic corrective. But the criticism did not so much repudiate empirical research itself as it did the paradigm of reality that the empirical outlook promoted and the industrialized society it created. For the romantics, knowledge is not simply explanation evoked from aggregates of facts; rather, it resembles "the swallow on the lake that sees and stirs the surface-shadow there but never yet hath dipt into the abysm" (Tennyson). And when the romantics took a close look at the new industrialized society, they announced that "the woods of Arcady are dead" (Yeats). And they noted the deicide of the French *philosophes*. "Pan is not here and will not come again. No horned faun treads the yellow leaves. No god at dawn steals through the olive trees" (Wilde). Mystery, felt intuition, nature, concreteness, totalities—these themes constitute the romantic corrective. If Newton symbolizes the Enlightenment's empiricist principle, Goethe fittingly represents the intuitive imagination.

To hear that religion, in this case Western Christianity, offered a corrective to the Enlightenment comes as no surprise. A quick review might be content to observe that the theologians reacted in self-defense and that theirs was a self-serving criticism. After all, the insistence that all human claims must be assessed challenges a faith that places its own doctrinal and moral tradition and its Scriptures beyond assessment on the grounds that they are the standards, the touchstones of criticism. The churches, Catholic and Protestant, did resist the Enlightenment, and this resistance and a fundamental ambivalence about the critical principle are still very much alive in modern Christendom. Nevertheless, we should not permit the self-serving nature of the churches' response to obscure the seriousness of the theological criticism. Like Romanticism, the theological corrective has not directly repudiated the critical principle or even its empiricist embodiment. Superficially viewed, the theological criticism challenges empiricism's sufficiency as a world view but not its efficiency as a method. Carrying the banners of Karl Barth, Paul Tillich, Rudolf Bultmann, and Karl Rahner, neo-orthodox theologians have appealed to revelation and redemption to expose the limitations of both the formal critical principle and the empiricist paradigm as a comprehensive metaphysic. I call this a superficial account of the theological corrective, because it pits the Enlightenment metaphysic against religious fideism, and that obscures the real criticism of the Enlightenment's critical principle. Beneath neo-orthodox polemics is an inheritance from Schleiermacher: the assumption that reason and tradition are mutually exclusive. And that is much the same mistake as the Enlightenment's supposition that its polemic against tutelage and prejudice has robbed tradition, the sedimentation of the historical experience of people and ages, of any possible function as a bearer of truth. It might be argued that the only way the Enlightenment could establish the formal critical principle was to win freedom from the authoritative institutions of its time, and to do this required invalidating the tradition those institutions fought to protect. But according to the theological corrective properly viewed, the idea that tradition cannot be a bearer of truth is arbitrary, and reason and tradition are not mutually exclusive. The philosophy and sociology of science today argue that all knowledge occurs in conjunction with deposits and strands of tradition, and this includes the sciences. The theological corrective makes a more aggressive point: that the corporate experience of past ages and peoples can produce a wisdom that is illuminating and pertinent beyond the past. If this is true, the task of knowledge is confronted not just by facts about the present to be explained but by sediments of past culture to be interpreted. Hence, this corrective recalls instruments born especially in the Renaissance which assist the interpretation of texts.

The third corrective of the Enlightenment is a radicalizing of criticism. Enlightenment criticism is scientific criticism. It occurs as an undertaking of pure reason carried out by people who want to know, whose passions are aroused by problems, perplexities, even mysteries. The Enlightenment hoped these struggles would produce a just society. The Enlighteners assumed that knowledge itself was an innocent means to that end. In the beginning, they asserted, is pure reason, the necessary instrument of all other undertakings. For the third corrective, however, in the beginning is not reason but power. There is no pure reason, only cognitive endeavors in service of whatever is in power in the society. By forgetting this, the institutions of pure reason—the sciences, scholarship, the universities—hide from themselves their complicity in societal agendas of power. Reason thus remains uncritical about its own complicity in the unjust society. It follows that the primary perspective and starting point of a genuine critical principle cannot be innocent reason but must be praxis.

We are familiar with the movements and literatures of this third corrective: Karl Marx, the social gospel, the Frankfurt school, black and feminist theologies, liberation theology. Like romanticism, the praxis movements correct Enlightenment abstraction by a turn to the concrete. The romantic's concrete is formulated aesthetically, with a focus on the experiencing individual; the praxis concrete is the political-historical situation. Like the theological corrective, the praxis corrective highlights the past, the effects of tradition, the social dimension, but the focus is on communities cemented in oppressive structures that would close down possible change. Like the theological corrective, praxis is a hermeneutic insisting on the interpretive and perspectival character of knowledge, but the aim of the hermeneutic is to raise the moral consciousness, purge oppressive languages, uncover hidden oppressive agendas. That is why the third corrective is a radical version of the critical principle.

The Marginality of Corrected Knowledge

We are heirs to the Enlightenment. But what we have inherited is not just the formal critical principle and the empiricist paradigm of scholarship but also the subsequent correctives that the Enlightenment itself made possible. These too are part of our history. We shall call this total heritage the Enlightenment tradition. And this tradition is very much a part of the contemporary world and even the university. To understand the fragility and corruptibility of knowledge in the university, we need to explore just how this tradition, the Enlightenment and its correctives, is present now in the university.

Two convictions guide my interpretation of this presence. The first is that the correctives are more than simply past movements that titillate the historian's curiosity. Because they occur as correctives to an approach to knowledge and as such are themselves interpretations of what critical knowledge is, they make claims on us. More than that, each of the correctives may hold a truth about something. The empirical strand of the Enlightenment professes the primary status of facts and events and the inescapability of specific abstracting and focusing inquiry. The romantic corrective holds before us the complexity, the multidimensionality of each thing that is real, exposing thereby the cognitive violation that every abstracting inquiry commits. The theological corrective recalls that, as David Tracy says, historical experience of a people can produce classic texts—that knowledge occurs in conjunction with the reinterpretation of historically engendered deposits of wisdom. Knowledge is not totally separated from anamnesis, the remembering of peoples. The praxis hermeneutic uncovers the ideological and political character of all human knowledge.

Altogether, these three correctives describe the complexity of reality and therefore the complex character of knowledge. They illumine the dimensions of knowledge and expose how knowledge can be distorted when it reduces itself to single paradigms. If the correctives are serious accounts of the complexity of knowledge, the critical principle cannot be simply the formal principle about the unrestricted scope of assessment. In its correctives the Enlightenment tradition embodies but goes beyond the formal critical principle. And criticism and critical knowledge are diminished by the absence of any one of these correctives. The correctives expand what we have called the Enlightenment ideal beyond the formal principle and even beyond its empiricist principle to include the intuitive imagination, tradition, and praxis. In other words, knowledge has an uncritical character when it loses connection with the intuited concrete, with the mediations of tradition, and with the determinations of social power.

The second conviction is that none of these approaches is by itself an adequate account of knowledge and of the programs of science and scholarship. We can put it stronger. Each approach by itself distorts knowledge by suppressing the complexity of reality. Empirical method has stunning success in understanding very specific causal relations. When isolated from all correctives, it loses the concrete reality in its complexity and, with this, the conditions of criticizing itself. Isolated, it tends to become a paradigm of reality itself, but of reality without the social and political contexts of knowledge, reality dispersed into abstract formulas or casual sequences, reality absented from the deposits of the past's wisdom. The romantic corrective latches on to organic metaphors to reveal the mysteries of things. Isolated, it ends up as an aestheticism, indifferent to the powers of the social order and the technologies of human survival. The theological corrective, always nervous before the unrelenting impress of the critical principle, by itself is prone to reduce knowledge to a relation to the authoritative past. The bearer of wisdom, namely, tradition, becomes itself the evidence for truth. The questers of truth are turned into vendors of interpretation. The lantern of Diogenes will not stop here. Praxis isolated becomes a situational abstraction. Cut off from the wisdom of the past and the rigors of empiricism, it becomes a pragmatics of action easily degenerating into a fanaticism without norms and motivation.

What then is the present status of the Enlightenment tradition? The various correctives of the Enlightenment have persisted into the present age but with little power to exercise their corrective function. The paradigm of knowledge and reality that now reigns is an offspring of Bacon and Newton. Its reign follows from its success, for it is just this very precise mathematical and technological instrument that has virtually created the modern world. It reigns because almost all of our military, economic, industrial, and even leisure and aesthetic activities depend on it. The point here is not to sing one more dirge about the sciences and the humanities or the perils of technology. I am talking about a paradigm, a model of knowledge that works better for some sciences than others but that has expanded to most of the specialty fields constituting the social sciences and humanistic scholarship. According to this model, understanding occurs as the result of concentrating research upon a very specific aspect of something.

There is nothing wrong with specialized research in itself. But it is one among many possible paradigms of knowledge. It did evoke the correctives we describe. Where are the correctives now? If the research paradigm is the chief executive officer, what is the status of these employees? The correctives of the Enlightenment are present in the modern world as dispersed movements that, relative to the reigning paradigm, are not corrective, supplemental, and central but competitive, polemical, and marginal. They are marginal because they have very little social and institutional support. That is to say, the modern versions of the correctives of imagination, tradition, and praxis are not sciences or even university disciplines. They do not have their home in university departments. They have few scholarly guilds and receive only modest support by foundation and government grants. Of course, obscured. What happens to knowledge and to scientific and scholarly undertakings when these interpretive perspectives are lost?

The restraint of the *intuitive imagination* may cause the most problems, because without it the other hermeneutic perspectives fail to emerge. For it is the intuitive imagination—that central theme of romanticism—which grasps reality in its concreteness, its relationalities, its complexity. Its correction is the uncovering of the immediate and concrete entity. In Wallace Stevens's words, "The squirming facts exceed the squamous mind." Analysis and research select certain facts and closely scrutinize them. But for the intuitive imagination those facts continue to squirm. The intuitive imagination grasps the other human being not as an aggregate of extracted data but as a core of experiencing and as a physical being, a being in social relations to others, a self-reflective way of being temporal. Intuitive imagination is not itself research nor can it displace research. But without it research develops tunnel vision and becomes the victim of its own abstraction. With it research is ever correcting itself by turning attention to other dimensions of its subject matter. Without it scholarship develops the illusion that its studied data are the reality. With it scholarship can correct itself by returning to the unabstracted and specific entity. Without the intuitive imagination's grasp of the immediacy and complexity of reality, other hermeneutic perspectives remain undeveloped. For it is the concrete, actual, interrelational thing that has dimensions of tradition and that reflects situations of political power.

What happens when knowledge takes place under the Enlightenment assumption that truth excludes *tradition?* What happens when past historical epochs, peoples, mythoi, and texts are repudiated as authoritarian dangers to pure reason? When we consider what the Enlightenment was up against, we have to respect the reasons behind such a repudiation. It was the price that had to be paid in defense of the formal critical principle. But it was a high price. Lost sight of in the transaction was the difference between the assertion of truth on precritical or authoritative grounds and the discovery of truth in the experiences of peoples of the past. Human communities large and small can experience and embody reality in insights more perduring than their provincial spaces and times. These communities have produced comprehensive myths, profound metaphors, classic texts that expose the frailties and possibilities typical of human beings in history.

Judaism, Buddhism, Catholic Christianity, and Protestant Christianity have poured into the stream of history a textual record of experience which has the ring of truth and insight. The tradeoff the Enlightenment made for a freely operative critical principle was the misprizing of all of that, on the grounds that myths are subterfuges for precritical authority.

When scholarship in a university buys into the repudiation of tradition, the only way it can entertain the past and its communities is by phenomenal description. The myths and insights of tradition are taken as proper objects of study in the university but only as data: biographies of the metaphysical poets, economic backgrounds of the Boer War, the sand paintings of the Navahos. Any move beyond this phenomenalism is assumed to be improper advocacy. Here we have the irony of disciplines that live in imitation of the hard sciences but that refuse to do what those sciences themselves insist on—that is, to assess the phenomena in their claims, their truth, their reality. Why is it that one can investigate and teach what is the case about amino acids and not about the Buddhist theme of suffering? The question conducts us back to the assumption that historical tradition cannot be truth bearing. This is why it is thought that tradition can be studied descriptively but not normatively—and therefore not at the point at which it might evoke a serious response, the point where it exerts a claim.

What we are describing as attenuated knowledge in the university parallels what Phillip Rieff calls a therapeutic, cultureless society. Here we have a society unable to grant any cognitive status to its past, and to the extent that it cannot, it has no real restrictions, guiding laws, genuine pieties. The Victorian poet Swinburne's description of the Jews in exile may describe our own time: "And they knew not their forefathers, nor the hills and streams and words of power."

What happens when the pure reason of research and scholarship oppose themselves to the corrective of praxis and its hermeneutics? A lesser consequence is a certain naive relation of knowledge to itself. The scholar is by nature immersed in the specific project held within the specialist's tunnel vision. One of the things the tunnel vision misses is the way the specialty is servile to larger societal struggles. All human activities occur in contexts, and most of them in contexts that are social and institutional. Cognitive activity is no exception, serving as it does educational, governmental, and privately incorporated institutions.

Cognitive undertakings that fail to embody the several dimensions of knowledge will pursue these tasks innocent of the way the results affect and are affected by powers at large.

Naiveté concerning the sociology of knowledge is a minor consequence of isolation. A major consequence is the abstraction perpetrated by a knowledge emptied of praxis considerations. I am not referring to the scholar's limitations that confine research to selected specialties, nor to the banal fact that no one can know everything. Rather, scholarship without the praxis hermeneutic systematically excludes a whole dimension of reality. We become aware of the systematic exclusion when we find our work corrected by someone who has applied a praxis perspective to what we ourselves have studied. For instance, historians of medicine who have construed the history of medical discovery to be their subject matter are introduced to a new world on reading Michel Foucault's *Birth of the Clinic*. American church historians are surprised to discover that the standard church histories virtually omit black religion and the black church. That exclusion attests not simply to a failure to treat certain subjects such as women and minorities but to a way of construing the subject matter itself, church history. In short, the praxis hermeneutic focuses on and uncovers a certain dimension of reality that, when considered, modifies the understanding of all the other dimensions. For this reason the praxis hermeneutic cannot be dismissed as false advocacy and an ideological endangerment to objective scholarship. As a corrective it exposes the ideological character already inherent in so-called objective scholarship.

The argument here is not with empiricism itself. It is with a one-dimensional conception of scholarship and science, a reduction of the critical principle to the empiricist paradigm alone. The systematic exclusion of imaginative, tradition-oriented, and praxis perspectives has helped produce a contemporary scholarship that is specialized to the point of triviality, preoccupied with technologies of method and with reworking already surfeited subjects with ever more ingenious procedures. Furthermore, in the modern university, the marginality of the Enlightenment correctives and the anorexic form of the critical principle have been socially and institutionally reinforced by the specialty fields, whose journals and guilds embody the paradigm and cooperate with the university's reward system to enforce it. In such a situation, knowledge, always fragile, is distorted. And its distortion is due to an arbitrary narrowing of the critical principle so that it no longer reflects the sense of the total Enlightenment tradition. Why does fragile knowledge become distorted knowledge? The critical principle itself, even in the full sense of a synthesis of all these correctives, provides no explanation. This problem presses us beyond the Enlightenment heritage to what may be a more radical version yet of the critical principle. And that is the subject of chapter 2.

18   Theology and University Education

are no exception. We too are struggling, striving beings. What is more, there is a certain self-consciousness about our striving and about our opposition to what frustrates our aims and activities. And although all human activities, even very spontaneous ones, indicate purposes and aims, some of them get our attention more than others. We are more exercised over a debilitating illness than over a lost book in the library.

Since the time of Plato and Aristotle people have argued that one of the not so trivial traits of human beings is a basic desire and striving to know. A renowned historian of philosophy at Columbia University, John Herman Randall, Jr., had a Groucho Marx–like rejoinder to this: "Aristotle," he said, "never had the privilege of teaching in an American university." But that does not lay the issue to rest. At the everyday level, knowledge is a grasp of how things in our environment work, so as to enable us to carry out various aims. Going to work, cooking a meal, shopping, reading, driving a car, working a stereo system all involve knowledge. In this sense every human being needs to know, wants to know, and knows. And yet the matter does not end with knowledge in the service of everyday aims. Even the everyday world presents to the human being all sorts of perplexing problems, and to solve one is to open up ten others. Furthermore, something about the human being is drawn to what is confusing and mysterious and finds satisfaction when the problem is solved, the mystery illumined. I do not want falsely to universalize the matter. My aim here is less the empirical determination of the proportion of human beings who desire to know, and to what degree, than it is to make a point about knowledge itself. Knowing is an activity, and this activity expresses a rather basic desire. And like other basic desires—for instance, the desire to be, to survive, to be with the other in modes of affection, to experience pleasure or the beautiful—the desire to understand does not have a restricted object, one thing or set of things such that, if known, the desire is satisfied. The desire to know is ever on the move. In the story of Faust the desire to know is intensely self-conscious, and the more Faust self-consciously tries to satisfy it, the more the satisfaction eludes him. This presents us with another meaning of the fragility of knowledge. Knowledge serves a desire that cannot, it seems, be finally satisfied. Elusiveness, frustration, and fragility are features that knowledge shares with other fundamental human desires, all of which take place in the context of the general fragility of human existence. There is a certain discontent about this very situation which prompts human beings to try to end that discontent. This brings us to the second stage of the exploration.

Corrupted Knowledge

With the second step we cross into another territory forbidden by the Enlightenment tradition in its narrowed form. Enlightenment criticism without its corrective by a tradition-oriented hermeneutic dismisses the past as not having cognitive significance. For it, truth may issue in predictions but not in retrievals from the past. Given that prejudice, the mythoi of world religions are out of bounds. We now step across the boundary to explore knowledge in the framework of the Christian mythos. We are here making a theological move. Let us hope it is not an uncritical move, a special pleading, or a mere appeal to authority.

Every form of human social life that I have ever heard of has identified ways in which human beings can go wrong: for example, by acting against the interests of the group (the tribe, the company), taking excessive revenge, brutally violating other people, or displaying exclusive attachment to material goods. All human communities in history have the conception of human deviations from the ideal or normative, the good, personal, and human. The Christian mythos offers a general portrayal of such deviations both in the form of an old theogonic story and in the form of a dynamics of human evil.

To uncover the dynamics of human evil we need to add to the picture of human beings as constituted by very basic and even distinctive strivings. I said that the basic human desires are never simply satisfied. We must add to this that human desire has a tragic character. It is not only that it occurs in a fracture between desire and desired which is never closed but that the situation of human desiring is the organic and historical situation of physical, social, and personal peril. The peril is not merely a possibility or an occasional accident but the very structure of organic-historical life. Human beings strive in the face of an unknown future, in the mode of constant uncertainty, in the midst of things constantly going wrong. "In the shadow of the hawk we feather our nests," says Edna St. Vincent Millay.

It is not a tolerable situation. When we see the hawk's shadow, we not only feather our nests, we reinforce them with tons of steel and cement. Finding the hawk's shadow intolerable, we insist on being secured. But we want more than the relative safety provided by locked doors, new marvels of pharmacology, and better weapons systems. For the hawk flies over all these things, and we know it. Because peril and pain are intolerable, human beings are not content with the relative protections of the everyday world. We push on to what will secure absolutely, what will eliminate the hawk altogether. What is that? It is any and all goods, any and all relative protections regarded as invulnerable and able to secure. The various desires that have no final and fixed object now find an object. The whole restless, seeking life of the human being is driven by an insistence that the intolerable tragic dimension disappear and that there be protections that really and fully and absolutely protect. All good and functioning things become potential removers of the tragic. So we human beings seek out and attach ourselves to the perfect mate, the perfect educational institution, national heritage, political party, composer, school of thought, cognitive method. And this sort of attachment has a radically corrupting effect on the human being. The reason is that it corrupts the desires themselves. They are transformed from desires occurring on an ever-open horizon into desires pretending to possess their insisted-on satisfactions. The Grail search is thus brought to an end.

The trouble is that what has fulfilled the desires always itself has a tragic dimension and is threatened by a thousand perils. So the human being does whatever is necessary to protect the protector—to defend it, to justify it, to dehistoricize it, to rewrite its past, to purge it of all vulnerability and ambiguity. And so arise postures of envy, malice, and xenophobia that produce absolute enemies and justify every kind of assault on them. Human beings will become anything, do anything, join anything if it promises to remove the shadow of the hawk.

According to the Christian mythos, these are the dynamics of human evil. Now, in the old story the ancestors of the human race lost their innocence by disobeying a divine interdict. And our account of the dynamics of evil has said nothing at all about God. Yet the Christian mythos's interpretation of human evil is what Richard Niebuhr called a radical monotheism. Expressed negatively, it says that the horizon of human strivings—infinite, undesignated, negative—can never be identified with anything actual, anything constituted by us as a protection. There can be no identity between the network of beings and the mystery of that network, between creation and creator. Expressed as an imperative, it says, "You shall have no other gods before me."

Theonomous Criticism

The Enlightenment tradition has provided us with not one but two principles of criticism. The formal critical principle asserts that human knowledge is never exempt from further investigation and assessment. This principle is based on the recognition that all actual things are both temporal and relative, and hence that all knowledge of actual things must be continually corrected as states of affairs change and as evidence adapts to different perspectives. In addition to the formal principle are conceptions of knowledge that express paradigms of reality: empiricist, intuitive-imaginative, tradition-oriented, and praxis-oriented. The three correctives of the empiricist paradigm constitute a second principle of criticism: the hermeneutic principle that knowledge involves a series of interpretive shifts. Grounding this principle is the fact that all actual things are multidimensional. This second principle goes beyond the correction of arbitrary authority by more specific research to the interpretation of other dimensions of the reality under consideration.

The thesis of the present chapter is that the Christian mythos engenders a third type of criticism and a third critical principle. But we need to head off several misunderstandings that such a thesis invites. First, I am not talking about a criticism that the Christian religion directs to the so-called secular world. We are all aware that the Christian religion itself is a prime example of cognitive idolatries, of the erection of a house of absolute knowledge and a denial of the historical character of wisdom. But we should not let the Enlightenment's ruthless exposure of Christian idolatries shelter from exposure the general tendency of human beings to secure themselves in their cognitive paradigms; we must not forget the many other absolutized cognitive houses that continue to be erected.

Second, I do not want to argue that the third critical principle is borne exclusively by the Christian mythos. It is, I think, part of the deep structures of that mythos, but there are forms of it in other faiths. Finally, I am not saying that this third type of criticism is a possession of theologians in the sense of being made available only in theological literature using theological methods. Its genre is instead very much like that of the first two critical principles, which are not so much discrete methods as general postures that inform institutions, communities, and the perspectives of individuals.

The term "Christian mythos" refers, following Bernard Meland's definition, to "the pattern of meaning which arises from the structured experience of a people and having to do with the ultimate nature and destiny of human being."[1] How is it that something like that might engender a posture of criticism? First, the Christian mythos creates an orientation to and seriousness about reality. We should not let the Inquisition's treatment of Renaissance scientists and the anti-intellectualism of modern popular religion mislead us. In many epochs the Christian movement has attached itself to the going interpretation of reality, cosmos, and world process, whether Platonic, Aristotelian, Newtonian, or some other. Nihilism, the co-conspirator of every true anti-intellectualism, is about as close as one can get to an opposite of the Christian mythos. Faith affirms reality, because it experiences everything that is theonomously, sacramentally, and in relation to a mystery through which things have being.

Second, a vision of corruption and redemption is the heartbeat of the Christian mythos. The Christian mythos combines a theonomous understanding of reality with a radical conception of the corruption of human history and the possibilities of redemption. How then do these motifs constitute an interpretation of knowledge?

When we view knowledge through the lens of the Christian mythos, what do we see? We see the human being acting in a certain way, striving to end various perplexities and confusions. We see the striving to know, and we see it occurring under the shadow of the hawk. None of the elemental strivings of human beings is separate from the inability to tolerate the shadow and from the insistence on being secured against all tragic structures; the striving to know and understand participates in that insistence. The hawk's shadow terrorizes us into wanting more, insisting on more. And we end up transforming knowledge into an idol that can satisfy desire absolutely, into a securing power. This entails something more subtle than a so-called trust in reason or the pedant's effete erudition. Few modern idolatries of knowledge take those forms. But the idolatry of knowledge always has as at least one feature the occupation of the house of knowledge in an undialectical way. By calling it undialectical, I mean that a liberation from naive, precritical, or dogmatic knowledge has come about in such a way that the paradigm that effected the liberation is taken as the one thing able to deliver reality to the knower. Undialectical knowledge sees human history as stumbling about in the fogs of myth and superstition for thousands of years only now to emerge into the light. It sees schools of science and philosophy as having perpetrated all sorts of confusions and naivetés until matters were finally straightened out with Heidegger's *Being and Time*, or symbolic logic, or the Apple II, or deconstruction, or Sigmund Freud—so that now there is the end, that is, the fulfillment, of philosophy and science. Of course the end of theology has long been proclaimed, both in the sense of a termination and in the sense of a fulfillment. Ironically, radical criticism of a certain kind obscures from itself its own absolutization. Thus some corrective modes of thought that announce themselves to have replaced almost all cognitive enterprises of past and present are almost completely undialectical, with virtually no self-transcendence.

The criticism of knowledge engendered by the Christian mythos is not reducible to an exposure of corrupted knowledge. One of the consequences of the corruption of knowledge is the abandonment of knowledge. The abandonment of knowledge is deeper than the loss of the formal critical principle, since it is at the same time a turning away from reality. A kind of reality loss occurs whenever we do very refined and specific research. If the object of our abstraction is permitted to be the reality, abandonment begins, both by a loss of the total entity and by sheer methodological determination of the nature of the entity. When the specific paradigm of knowledge is placed beyond any dialectical correction, this state of affairs is frozen. The more our cognitive undertakings move toward the technical, toward the methodological, and toward the uses of knowledge in pursuit of power, the more indifferent they become to questions of reality.

According to faith's portrayal of the dynamics of evil, this is an expected outcome, since whenever the human striver puts the achievement of absolute security from the shadow of the hawk onto its agenda, it builds radical failure into its whole program. If we expect the Enlightenment tradition to remove the shadow, we expect too much. It turns out that the true philosophy, the Freudian hermeneutic, the stunning technologies do not deliver. And when they do not, the cognitive temper that impelled us to seek them drives us to cynicism about the cognitive endeavor itself. We may still occupy our cognitive houses but with other than interests in reality.

In the corruption and abandonment of knowledge is manifest the essential instability of knowledge. The Christian mythos engenders a criticism directed at both sides of this instability. It offers a posture that combines an interest in what is real and an interpretation of the corruption and redemption of all that is real. Compared with the formal critical principle and various hermeneutical corrections, this is a third posture of criticism. Is this third criticism itself a hermeneutic, to be added to those of intuitive imagination, tradition, and praxis? I do not think so. The reason is that the hermeneutic correctives are created by the dimensions of real things. But what are set forth in the Christian mythos are less dimensions of reality than simply reality's corruptive and redemptive possibilities. The third principle is not so much a hermeneutic as a critical posture in which certain convictions, suspicions, and even hopes operate.

Furthermore, this critical posture is not a matter of just the human *individual's* cognitive life. Knowledge itself may be an act of the individual, but that act occurs in conjunction with historical accomplishments, institutions, and corporate undertakings. Therefore, the corruption and abandonment of knowledge are a matter not simply of human individuals but of epochs, cultures, institutions, and schools. Accordingly, the theological critical posture needs embodiment not just in the intentional life of individuals but in communities of knowledge.

Corrupted Correctives

One final question: How is the theological critical posture related to the correctives of the Enlightenment? Each of these correctives constitutes a potential criticism of the other correctives when they become self-sufficient and isolated. The independence or isolation of the correctives is not the issue posed by the Christian mythos. Rather, the issue is an idolatrous knowledge, which drives human cognitive endeavors to isolation and results in an undialectical view of knowledge. Further, the Christian mythos sees cognitive endeavors as not only distorted by isolation but also corrupted by self-absolutization. Hence, each of the four correctives of critical knowledge is vulnerable to corruptions that are not just the results of their isolation from the others.

What happens to the empiricist paradigm when idolatrously it becomes *the* answer to knowledge's fragile striving—when it becomes a cognitive dwelling that secures the human being absolutely? In the absence of other correctives it rests content with its abstraction and with its cognitive successes. As an absolutized paradigm, empiricism moves beyond its own area of genius, the focused investigation, and spawns a world view, a life posture, a reigning discourse, even a type of society. In that society the procedures that work so well in focused research engender discourse that sets the tone for various bureaucracies, for mental hospitals, human services, government agencies, and universities. Empiricism pretends to, but does not succeed at, the quantification of the realities with which these communities have to do. As a world view, it can offer only its research methods and the aggregate of data that its methods have made possible, both of which are quickly commandeered by the prevailing societal powers.

What happens to the intuitive imagination when it turns its own genius and corrective into the ultimate weapon against the hawk? We are familiar with the results, because the modern form of distorted imagination may be what Phillip Rieff calls the therapeutic society and what Christopher Lasch calls the culture of narcissism.[2] Turned in on its own operation, the imagination loses connection with the wisdom of the past. The result is experience without judgment, being oneself without being with or for the other, belief without truth, spirituality without discipline. The intuitive imagination loses reality too, indifferent as it is to whatever does not promote or support its inwardness.

The tradition-oriented corrective tries to restore the past as a bearer of wisdom. We are all familiar with what happens when tradition denies its own fragility and constructs powerful institutions to maintain its denial. Tradition ceases to be a bearer of wisdom inviting each new generation to an interpretive reappropriation and assessment but becomes a cognitive given, offering itself as the norm for all assessments. Maintained in power, its institutions will then punish those who question its transcritical givenness. When the fragility of tradition and knowledge is denied, we have not simply an isolation but a repudiation of the formal critical principle. The Enlightenment recognized this and identified religion as reason's first enemy. Marx echoed this sentiment in his oft-quoted dictum that "the criticism of religion is the premise of all criticism." The idolatry of tradition is the characteristic corruption of religion, for the understandable reason that religious knowledge occurs in conjunction with the community's stored wisdom. But the idolatry of tradition is not merely a religious idolatry. It infects all forms of human society which determine the present by citing the normative past. Thus any nation, culture, subculture, or organized group can come to regard what it inherits from the past as an uncriticizable given.

We are familiar also with the corruptions of the praxis hermeneutic. In itself that hermeneutic is a radical correction of all cognitive agendas that support structures of social injustice by ignoring them. But when it is laid hold of as having no fragility, it develops its own grand inquisitors. Its advocacy of the oppressed becomes a privileged position immune from criticism. External critics are excluded by reason of their location outside the oppressed situation. Internal critics are repudiated as disloyal to the cause. When the praxis agenda inflates itself into something all-inclusive and absolute, all behavior on its behalf is thought justified. The fallibility of its cognitive claims is removed by the politics of oppression. By this stage the praxis hermeneutic has degenerated into totalitarian and fanatical forms. In corrupted praxis, power acquires not only a priority over knowledge but comes to determine knowledge. And the end of this road is, as with the other correctives, a subjugation of knowledge and the loss of reality.

From the perspective of the Christian mythos, these corruptions are not simply the effects of the failure of the corrections, the results of a narrowed hermeneutic. They do not even describe the fragility of knowledge itself but describe rather fragility denied. The Enlightenment tradition saw the threat to knowledge posed by absolutized tradition, and it fought for the liberation of pure reason through pure reason. It did not, it seems, grasp the essential corruptibility of knowledge, and therefore, of its own embodiments of pure reason.

In sum, the Enlightenment tradition includes both the original Enlightenment corrective and subsequent correctives of the Enlightenment, but the various correctives constituting the second hermeneutic principle of criticism never came together to form a single ideal of critical reason but survived in relative independence one from the other. These correctives are present in the university only at the margin of the paradigm that sets the standards for science and scholarship. Thus the hermeneutic correctives have not had a great influence on the university, and what influence they have had may now be lessening as scholarship is splintered into ever more narrowly defined fields. Insofar as the tradition-oriented corrective has only marginal standing in the university, there is little awareness there of a third and radical critical posture borne by the Christian mythos which would disclose the unstable combination of corrupted knowledge and abandoned knowledge in the Enlightenment tradition itself.

Our conclusion is a question: How is it possible for an element from a religious mythos to be at all pertinent to a university? The university's formal critical principle was hard won, and the battle left the conviction that knowledge can be freely pursued only if the university does not subject itself to tradition, religious or otherwise. That conviction reflects the Enlightenment's tendency to view reason and tradition as mutually exclusive. But subjection to a tradition's authority and critical retrieval of a tradition's wisdom are surely two different things, with the latter not at all at odds with reason. When the tradition-oriented hermeneutic is not suppressed, there can take place a retrieval of wisdom from the various ages, cultures, and literatures of the past. And modern students can then continue to be shaped by East and West, by Isaiah and Homer, by Thomas Aquinas and Sigmund Freud.

Part of the heritage shaping us is the Christian mythos and its portrayal of the corruptibility of historical existence. Applied to fragile knowledge, this portrayal may be not a quaint dogmatic but a widely applicable insight into how things are. The insight can effect a critical posture without being a belief in a doctrine. If human beings in history do in fact perpetuate idolatries and if these idolatries exploit the fragility of knowledge, surely the university—the community of knowledge—is impoverished if it settles for a naiveté that excludes that possibility. If the third critical posture can have some presence and manifestation, a way may be opened not only for the correctives but for the redemption of human knowledge.

NOTES

1. Bernard Meland, *Fallible Forms and Symbols: Discourses on Method in a Theology of Culture* (Philadelphia: Fortress Press, 1976), 102; Meland is quot-

3

The Fragmentation of Knowledge: Specialty Fields and the University

Undergraduate and graduate teaching in the university is organized by cognitive specialties. Oriented primarily toward research, these specialties are shaping the university for both good and ill. There are even signs that research does not prosper under them.[1] Chapters 1 and 2 set the problematic character of the university against a historical background and argued that the suppression of important correctives in the Enlightenment tradition has resulted in paradigms of knowledge, understanding, and inquiry that are too narrow. The present chapter carries the exploration another step. It moves beyond the historical legacy that shapes the university to the institutional embodiment of that legacy in specialism. The thesis is that many of the problems of the university can be traced to the social entity research-oriented universities have created as the instrument of inquiry and teaching: the specialty field. The cognitive and pedagogical efforts of the university have always been to some degree distributed among departments of learning. This chapter is about the current state of the perennial tension between the focused accuracy of specialization and the synthetic relationality that figures in the historical ideals of the university—a tension that reality itself forces on us. With the ascendancy of specialization over the ideal of synthetic relationality, there seems today to be a significant reduction of this tension; and that is a situation fraught with danger for the university.

What I present here is not a "study" but an interpretation informed by my experience of what is happening in the university and guided by a perspective I share with many there. There are scholars whose occupation of specialty fields so insulates them from the historical legacy and larger institutionality of the university that they will not recognize as a problem what I lament here. Most of the university's constituencies will, however, recognize what I am describing.

A thesis like mine calls for some disclaimers. It is not another tale of the sciences against the humanities. The humanities may, in fact, be more severely afflicted by the problem than the sciences are. It is not a repudiation of the idea and existence of scholarly specialties as such but a criticism of their present social reality. And it is not simply a repetition of the charge that the university has lost its unity,[2] for the loss of unity seems to be at present the university's unavoidable fate. The thesis, rather, is that the university is losing a tension that genuine knowledge requires—the tension between focused, cognitive abstraction and synthetic, relational correction—and that this loss is promoted by the hegemony of the specialty fields. I shall explore this thesis in three steps: first, in sorting out the vocabulary for distinguishing between sciences, disciplines, and pedagogical areas; second, in describing the social entity of the specialty field; and finally, in critically assessing the role of specialty fields in the current malaise of the university.

Sciences and Disciplines

What exactly is a specialty field? The question is crucial because of the almost overwhelming power and status bestowed by the idealizing nomenclature that the university uses to interpret its compartmentalization of knowledge. Since all institutions pursue their aims under concepts that are normative, there is nothing exceptional about the university's employment of idealizing nomenclature. What legitimates the professional existence of the scholar-teacher is a specialized responsibility for knowing and teaching. The scholar-teacher labors in the university only as representing a science, a discipline, a teaching area. But it is important to remember that the university's normative nomenclature is not empirically descriptive of the actual social groupings that organize the teaching and scholarly life of the university. Accordingly, the first task we face is to sort out the nomenclature and propose some working definitions to help identify the new entity on the scene, the specialty field.

Science and the Sciences

What is a science? In the United States the term "science" tends to be restricted to research and experiment, with natural science being the model that would-be sciences are to follow. In a broader usage a science is any collective cognitive (reality-oriented) undertaking that focuses on a selected or abstracted aspect of things and whose methods are appropriate to the kind of thing under consideration.[3] Because a science is a cognitive undertaking, its successful outcome involves some resolution of what is cognitively problematic. Any account of problem resolution is arbitrarily narrow if it is dominated by a single paradigm of reality and knowledge—for example, if it views all reality as events to be explained, structures to be described, repeatable actions to be predicted. Selecting or focusing is inevitable to any post–common-sense and rigorous knowing, and focusing is inevitably an abstracting, not in the sense of being speculative but in the sense of lifting out an aspect of something that is itself complex, interrelational, contextual, intrarelational, and in perpetual change. Because science is a focused or abstracting inquiry, no one method or paradigm can be adequate to knowing reality in its total complexity.[4]

Because focusing or abstracting is necessary to rigorous cognitive inquiry, there is a sense in which science has a tragic character: it can make cognitive headway only by a distortion of its object. Any abstracting act necessarily suspends consideration of the total concrete entity, its total context and environment, and its essential unrepeatability over time. Any specific entity—an enzyme, a rural village, a human emotion—occurs as a synthesis of aspects and dimensions and in a vast web of relations. To pursue any cognitive problem—for example, why the crime rate in a rural village has increased by twenty percent in one year—is to place in suspension most of the entity's contents and relations. The tragedy lies in the essentially unresolvable tension between the abstracted or focused aspect and the synthetic (concrete) character of what is under consideration.[5] The cognitive posture of genuine science includes an awareness of this perpetual distortion, though it would not necessarily describe the distortion in this way. Hence, genuine science is inclined to correct the distortion by taking into consideration other aspects and dimensions. Genuine science is a perpetual self-correcting movement between the abstract and synthetic poles; in the correction, the inevitable abstracting of science is transcended.

A simplistic and common-sensical understanding of the complexity of entities may see abstract aspects and synthetic totalities in quantitative terms, as parts and wholes. Corrections guided by this understanding are made by moving to other parts: for example, when the question concerns the increased crime rate in the village, the move might be from an inquiry into the efficacy of certain law-enforcement practices to an inquiry into the influence of television violence. But everything actual is "dimensionally" complex.[6] Dimension, a category taken from spatial or space-time analyses, is at best a metaphor for the complexity under consideration. Think of time as a fourth dimension; here there is a dimensional shift beyond the three dimensions of space. Time is not simply something in the same genre as spatial relations. It is not simply another part of a whole. The complexity of the human being is also not simply a diversity of parts, apples and oranges in a box. The human being's intentional, emotional, and social life is not on the same dimensional plane as its enzymes. Of course, its emotions can be quantified, but not without a certain loss. If complexity is, in fact, dimensional, the correction of focused abstraction can and should be a dimensional correction. Such correction involves not just altered hypotheses of explanation but the development of *perspectival emphases*. Perspectival emphases originate in insights into the dimensions of an entity and involve new planes of interpretation. For example, the historian of early-nineteenth-century American utopian communities may move from internal phenomenological analysis of the community's corporate piety to political and economic studies. The correction here is a dimensional one that is prompted by insights occurring on a new plane.[7]

Map Sciences and Actual Sciences

Two theses are especially important to the argument of this chapter: the first affirms the social and historical nature of science; the second, the difference between sciences and disciplines. The first thesis is sometimes neglected because of an equivocation between sciences as ideal entities in a proposed or presupposed architectonic of sciences, and sciences as actual corporate projects. By an ideal or map science, I mean a discrete area of knowledge, methods, and procedures which can be situated on a comprehensive map of cognitive undertakings. A specific ideal science is legitimated by its presence on some cognitive map; the earliest such maps appear to have been offered by Plato and Aristotle. Most map systems include generic sciences (natural sciences, social sciences), sciences themselves (sociology, psychology), and subsciences or branches (molecular physics, ornithology). Most schemes classify the sciences on the basis of types or regions of subject matter and their correlative methods.[8]

By an actual science—which is on the other side of the equivocation—I mean an actual, corporate project, a cognitive exploration occurring in a historical situation, drawing on the past in a particular way, and dominated by paradigms of knowledge and reality. Actual sciences occur in contexts (industry, government, university) and have reinforcing collegial agencies (the learned society, the department).[9] Actual sciences are not necessarily unrelated to the map entities. Many an actual science embodies as its unity some science in a mapping classification of sciences. Others, however, may not reflect any one science on the map, since the historical process of the development of the sciences is not governed by any ideal structure of classification.

Given the distinction between map and actual sciences it cannot be simply presupposed that the latter admit of rigorous, rational definition. Even if map sciences must have certain formal characteristic features, there is no guarantee that any actual scientific group or project will embody those features.

Sciences, Pedagogical Areas, and Disciplines

There is a second equivocation that has perpetuated confusion in thinking about the organization of the sciences and the distribution of areas of learning in the university. This is an equivocation on the word "science" that allows some areas to think of themselves falsely as sciences. We must acknowledge that in everyday usage the terms "science" and "discipline" are frequently interchangeable.[10] Thus the equivocation that allows disciplines to call themselves sciences has a certain sanction in ordinary speech. Nevertheless, it is important to distinguish sciences and disciplines, simply because they are two different even if closely related phenomena. Moreover, the employment of two different terms to refer to the two different phenomena has a strong etymological warrant.[11] If science is corporate activity that focuses on a cognitively problematic region of reality using methods appropriate to that region, it presumably can exist in any environment or institution that permits it to pursue its task. The sciences have often found their home in environments of teaching and learning—this as far back as Plato's Academy and the medieval universities—but educational settings are not necessary. At the present time scientific and scholarly work occurs in many types of environments and institutions—governments, corporations, museums, institutes, schools. Teaching environments are proper, but not the exclusive, settings for scientific work.

What then is a discipline? The term "discipline" connotes instruction, teaching, learning. At the same time a discipline is clearly not simply an area of teaching. Learning depends on the sciences to provide it with its specific subject matters, and if the learning occurs in a school, the subject matters are organized into a curriculum. It would be a mistake, however, to think of disciplines as the distributed subject matters of any curriculum in any school. Selected areas of focused teaching in schools are *pedagogical areas*. But some pedagogical areas are disciplines and some are not. Although cooking, auto mechanics, and reading are all teaching areas in schools, they are not disciplines. A discipline is a pedagogical area that exists in a teaching and learning situation in which the teaching and learning are facilitated by the pursuit of scientific, scholarly inquiry. An educational or pedagogical environment is necessary to disciplines. And the kind of educational institution in which disciplines occur is one in which teaching and learning require ongoing scientific and scholarly work. The disciplinary divisions of such an institution will frequently serve as the basis for organizing the institution, and each of the disciplines will reflect the way ongoing scholarship founds its teaching.[12]

On the other hand, the educational aims even of schools of this sort—universities, many professional schools, all Ph.D.-level graduate programs—are usually sufficiently complex to require pedagogical areas that are not disciplines. Areas such as philosophy, religious studies, the humanities, and the fine arts may require scholarly work in conjunction with their teaching but will themselves not be disciplines.[13] That is because what unify these areas are not sciences or even groups of sciences but perspectival emphases. No abstracted "regions of reality" define the subject matters of such areas. So pedagogical areas often only distort their work and their teaching in their attempts to be sciences or disciplines or to partition themselves into sciences or disciplines.

I suggest that in their primary meaning, both "science" and "discipline" refer to actual social entities, not map entities. Because the context of my investigation is the university, my focus will be on disciplines, not sciences as such. I propose to conduct my investigation from a certain way of understanding the sciences, that is, as reality-oriented cognitive undertakings whose inevitable abstracting or focusing calls for constant correction. Since reality itself is dimensional and contextual, this correction involves ever-developing perspectival emphases.

The Rise of Specialty Fields

I am exploring the thesis that something about the social carriers of teaching and research in the university is now compromising the university's aims. To say that something is wrong with academic *disciplines* presupposes that disciplines have remained the primary social units of instruction. We must, however, be open to the possibility that disciplines are no longer the primary social agents of the university's endeavors. As we shall see, disciplines have in fact evolved into another kind of social unit, which I am calling the *specialty field*. My task is to describe what constitutes this new social entity and how it came about. We recall that sciences and disciplines always exist in specific historical situations and as embodiments of functions, powers, and societal values. The same thing is true of specialty fields, where by a "specialty field" I mean the social entity that has displaced disciplines, especially in research-oriented universities. Four historical conditions in fact combine in the making of the specialty field: these involve the professionalization of the scholar-teacher, the reward system of the modern university, the paradigm of narrowed empiricism, and the ascendancy of the isolated specialty. But only when the analysis is completed will it be clear why the social entity of the specialty field is neither a science nor a discipline.

The Professionalization of the Scholar-Teacher

The nineteenth-century upheavals that effected this nation's transition from a primarily agrarian culture with an expanding frontier to an urban and industrialized society existing in a global economy and politics stimulated cataclysmic changes in all of the nation's institutions. There was the rise of the various institutions of higher education: colleges, large private and public universities, professional schools, and graduate programs. There was also the nineteenth-century professionalization of many of the working activities of the American middle class. Impelling and shaping both professionalism and higher education were the industrialization of the society and the stunning technological achievements that made industrialization possible. Out of the merging of professionalization and the new sciences and higher education came the university as we now know it, in which the older classical education, with its generalist and learned professors, gave way to a multistage professional and graduate education conducted by a specialist professoriate.[14] The new industrial sciences, the post-Enlightenment methods of scholarship arriving from the European universities, and the training for new professions all required highly specialized cognitive endeavors. The new specializations were not the origin of the partitioning and distribution of knowlege and teaching in the university, since some such distribution characterized the universities from their inception. But in the past, professors who had been educated comprehensively in the two major organa of classical scholarship— ancient languages and logic—could be scholars and teachers across the lines of this distribution.

The nineteenth-century upheavals saw the beginning of what Burton Bledstein calls the culture of professionalism. According to Bledstein, the professionalization of various kinds of work was a means to upgrading them and to giving status to the emerging American middle class.[15] In his view, the university was the primary agent of professionalization, since it provided the training and the symbolic credentials for the professions. What must not be overlooked is that the university was not only an agent but a recipient of professionalization. The disciplines themselves underwent professionalization, and the new specializations embodying the methods of the industrial sciences and Enlightenment scholarship were to a degree a manifestation of this status-giving movement.

What precisely does "professionalization" mean, especially when applied to an academic area? When professionalization occurs, people who share the same line of work (teaching, counseling, burying the dead, practicing law) create a societally recognized organization that establishes and enforces common standards for preparation and qualification for that work, for admission to the organization, and for practice of the work. Hence, a profession requires from the larger society an acknowledgment of the normative character of its standards, an agreed-upon educational route to the practice of the profession, persisting symbols for membership in the organization (degrees, licenses), and a means of monitoring the practice of the profession. The universities became agents of professionalization because of the role they played in the education of professionals. They were themselves professionalized because of the need of the scholar-teachers themselves for publicly recognized standards of education, admission, and practice.[16]

On the other hand, even though university teaching as a whole displays the marks of a profession, it would be misleading to call the specialty fields professions. University teaching as a whole is a profession because there is an agreed-upon educational process, admission process, symbolization, and monitoring for all university teachers. Still, the specialty fields have undergone a certain degree of professionalization.[17] They have many of the social features of the professions, but they remain quasi professions because their professional status in the society as a whole depends upon their role in the university. The specialty fields show the signs of professionalization in two social entities reflecting and regulating their standards: the professional association and the graduate-school program. The professional association is a socially structured organization with a defined membership which perpetuates the specialty through refereed journals, regularly scheduled conferences, and sponsored scholarly projects. Often there is in addition to this public and official institution an unofficial but very influential network of collaboration, the "invisible college."[18] Something like an invisible college unites and supports circles of artists, poets, and novelists. Membership is not really defined, and organization is minimal. In the sciences these invisible colleges are "network[s] of productive scientists linking separate groups of collaborators within a research area."[19]

The program of graduate study is the second standard-setting social entity that gives signs of the professionalization of the specialty fields.[20] It presides over the educational route to the specialty and defines the specialty not simply in a formal sense—as a general subject matter (sociology or European history)—but in respect of its content, scope, paradigms, and accepted methods. In addition it presides over the process of moving from the graduate school to the academic post. Methodological or paradigm consensus and a shared conception of acceptable agendas operate in the social worlds of both the graduate programs and the associations and invisible colleges. In other words, the specialty fields operate with a "stock of knowledge at hand"[21] that defines accepted horizons of research and that can be the subject of a sociology of knowledge. Although the standard-setting social entities of the specialty fields may not receive the sort of official recognition that is customary for those of law and medicine, they create the cognitive and social environment that the members of the specialty take for granted.

The Reward System of the University

As the new social unit of cognitive and pedagogical activity in the university, the specialty field participates in the larger professionalized environment of higher education. The university has its own standards and has created its own reward system for entry and survival in the professorial profession. Its reward system has contributed to the evolution of the disciplines into specialty fields and functions now to maintain those fields. The social and cognitive features of the fields themselves, their isolation of method and agenda, and their narrow paradigms of knowledge and method are all reinforced as the university's reward system conducts the professor up the career ladder.

It is no secret that American colleges and universities differ enormously in their standards for tenure and promotion. Their standards are much alike on paper. In practice, however, some schools are casual, almost indifferent, in observing their standards concerning research and publication, while others, especially those with prestigious graduate programs, enforce standards to attract and hold the nation's leading scientists and scholars. I shall here be speaking only about those universities which preside over graduate education, since they set the ethos and paradigms that dominate the world of research and scholarship.

It is clear that the reward system in these universities is geared not to academic disciplines but to specialty fields. The process begins with the specialty orientation of the graduate program. Most graduate degrees require fairly broad exposure to a discipline, but even so they tend to be degrees not in a discipline itself—in one or other of those subject areas in which the university organizes its scientifically based pedagogical areas (English, history, religion, biology)—but in a branch or specialty of a discipline. The qualifying examination and dissertation tend to be specialty-focused. Graduate education as specialty education anticipates what research-oriented universities will require of the scholar-teacher they employ. Upon employment the scholar-teacher's tenure clock starts ticking and there will be six or so years to accumulate a research-based case for promotion. In research-oriented universities, the case must be built on published research and scholarship that is competitive with the published research of ranked scholars at similar universities. The research and scholarship are expected to be original, advancing the field, and rigorous, respected by leading scholars. It must be pursued in the time gaps left by teaching and other responsibilities. And it must be brought to fairly frequent publication in the initial five years. The young scholar thus tries to identify an area of scholarship in which specific problems can be researched and in which it is possible to become a leading authority even in the pre-tenured period. The kind of research and scholarship the tenure time clock promotes is very much that which the specialism of the graduate school has already anticipated: specialty research. Accordingly, the young scholar either continues the dissertation specialty or quickly locates a new and equally narrow specialty. Once tenure is obtained, the scholar-teacher continues to build up a corpus of specialty studies in order to achieve promotion to full professor. Thus, the reward system encourages the scholar-teacher to begin in and remain in a specialty field; it affords little or no chance to explore broader territories, alternate paradigms, or the contours of the discipline itself.[22]

Scholarship in Surfeited Specialties

Professionalization bestows on academic projects a kind of entelechy, an impetus toward public legitimation. The legitimating entities are refereed journals, collaborative groups, and professional associations. The entelechy is toward the professionalized specialty field. The socially legitimating entities constitute the external horizon of specialty fields; that is, through these entities, the field's scholarly work develops. At the same time an internal horizon operates in the specialty fields. The boundaries of the specialty field are established externally, but once the subject matter and paradigms of a specialty field are given external boundaries, scholars search for a province within the field to make their own. Because a specialty is in the nature of the case a highly restricted cognitive undertaking, the direction of inquiry is toward greater detail. It is intensive rather than expansive. In order to carve out a special niche, aspiring scholar-specialists must settle for scrutiny of narrower and narrower sets of problems. Here too is a kind of entelechy, but its direction is toward the end of an ever-narrowing tunnel. The result is a surfeiting of the specialty field.

Some subject areas are more prone to surfeiting than others. Specialties whose subject matters, though narrow, are constantly changing—for example, specialties concerned with the politics of Argentina or the nature of health-care delivery systems—are not necessarily pressed into this narrowing tunnel. Nor are sciences whose subject matters consist largely of undiscovered terrain. On the other hand, specialties with more or less fixed subject matters such as an ancient text or a Victorian poet may be surfeited by decades and even centuries of scholarly scrutiny. In these instances, the changing horizon of inquiry comes either from focusing on ever more specific details or from new perspectival emphases and paradigms of method. New paradigms, however, tend to arise only to the degree that standard-breaking institutions permit them.

Narrowed Empiricism as the Dominant Paradigm

So far the description of specialty fields has been largely formal; the focus has been upon the specialty fields' social features. If we stopped here, we would miss the very substance of these new agencies of scholarship and teaching, namely, the paradigm of reality, knowledge, and method they take for granted as normative and as defining legitimate scholarship. This paradigm enjoins not just the abstracting and focusing necessary to any rigorous cognitive endeavor but a particular way of construing and carrying out that focusing. The complexity and multidimensionality of anything actual require many different kinds of focusings and, hence, a variety of methodological paradigms: statistical, predictive, text-interpretive, inductive, logical-mathematical, and so forth. In the past two centuries, quantitative methods have met with remarkable success. They have produced the engineering and technological successes on which modern civilization depends for its physical and economic well-being and for its awesome capacity to engage in global military conflict on a hitherto unimaginable scale. The physical and engineering sciences have become the royalty of the sciences, because of their preciseness, utility, and actual progress. The industrial, governmental, and military powers that preside over modern life all depend on these sciences and on their continued progress. As a result, the quantitative sciences now set the paradigm for study and research, as well as for what reality is and how it is known. Since these sciences build on procedures that focus on specific, measurable entities whose internal structure and external behavior can be studied by introducing environmental variables, the result is the detailed knowledge of physical and genetic "building blocks" and processes of the universe. Such knowledge makes possible an astonishing application of science to problems of health, disease and injury, weaponry, transportation, and communication. Because of the range of the quantitative paradigm's success, there arises an almost irresistible impulse to find ontological implications in the paradigm—to see the paradigm as telling what reality itself is. One comes to see reality as fundamentally nothing more than specific, discernible (researchable), and measurable units of activity and structure. With this, the object of the abstracting or focusing act becomes conflated with the reality itself.

The physical and engineering sciences now reign in our society. The extent of their realm is shown by the fact that their paradigm of research and method—and of reality and knowledge—pervades and dominates the social sciences and humanistic scholarship. The social sciences reflect the paradigm when they limit their abstracting to a focusing on specific measurable units, such things as the referents of human acts—for example, beliefs determined by questionnaire—and behavior measurable as data. Humanistic scholarship reflects the paradigm when it construes its subject matter as discrete units—say, the images of color in a novel, the cluster of publicly visible facts and occurrences that form the surface of a past event. When the paradigm becomes an *ontological* paradigm, a paradigm of reality itself, its paradigmatic character will go into hiding. When reality is taken to be revealed in abstracted units of explanation, the complexity and dimensionality of reality will be excluded by a methodological decision. Since it is insight into the complexity of reality itself that exposes paradigms as limited and convictional, the postural character of narrowed em-

specialty fields as I have just described them. After all, are these fields not the vanguard of all real cognitive and technological advance? It cannot be denied that significant advances have occurred through these agencies of science and scholarship. Hence, I would avoid simply repudiating the specialties. Nor would I minimize their contribution. What is more, my criticism does not gainsay the university's real diversity: there are many ways that the university is constantly transcending specialism. Perhaps the target of my criticism is still in the making. But if so, it is so far along in the making that the ethos and structure of the "best" universities are dominated by the displacement of disciplines by specialty fields. And where the displacement is most pronounced, we find a corruption of genuine science and a compromise of the historical aims of the university.

The Impoverishment of Knowledge

The criticism of specialism is nothing new.[24] I reiterate that I am not criticizing a narrowing of focus that is built on an accumulated and disciplined method; that is necessary to any genuine science. What I describe as corrupting the aims of genuine science and scholarship are professionalized specialty fields dominated by a narrow empiricism.[25] This corruption, resulting in a kind of cognitive mediocrity, takes the form partly of an impoverishment of some scholarly projects and partly of an isolation of the specialty. The first question is how the paradigm of narrowed empiricism impoverishes scholarship. Two major effects, both of the utmost seriousness, stand out.

The impoverishing effects lie largely in what a narrowed empiricism suppresses. The problem arises not so much because of the quality of what this empiricism yields in social and humanistic sciences as because of what it excludes from inquiry. Actualities, realities, are complex not simply as wholes having parts but as entities constituted by dimensions and occurring in larger systems of ever-changing interrelations. The complexity of human beings involves various kinds of dimensions and relations: anatomical structures, overt behaviors, social relations, experienced emotions, socially mediated traditions. These pose different kinds of cognitive challenge and call forth different "hermeneutics." Human complexity is in fact indicated by the variety of departmental teaching areas in the university: history, philosophy, linguistics, physiology. Driven by the paradigm of narrowed empiricism, the differentiated areas of study transform their subjects into entities or units analogous to the units successfully studied in the physical and engineering sciences. Emotions become certain measurable behaviors, human evil the effect of a cluster of diseaselike causalities, a work of fiction an aggregate of researchable instruments employed by the author, religion something present in researchable texts. The result is a variety of research enterprises with a uniformity created by the imitation of the reigning cognitive paradigm.

What is suppressed by this imitation? In some cases it is simply the thing itself in its distinctive being, genre, or way of occurring. A novel is itself not simply an aggregate of authorial instruments. An interpersonal relation—for example, between parent and child—is not simply a series of observable behaviors but a duration of reciprocal meaning-acts, intentions, and typifications. A historical event—for example, the French Revolution—is not simply a totality of datable occurrences. When the thing itself in its primary or essential genre is prevented from coming to view by methodological fiat, its dimensional and relational complexity will be missed. The restricting act that loses the thing itself and its dimensions will necessarily also lose sight of the many kinds of cognitive requirements—interpretive, exegetical, symbol analyzing, historical-genealogical—that these dimensions require.

With the suppression of dimensions, disciplines are redefined as ways of organizing specialties of one-dimensional inquiry. Eliminated or discredited in the university are teaching areas that have the character of perspectival emphases; these include philosophy, religious studies, and the fine arts. Thus perspectival emphases can no longer serve as correctives to the specialty fields. Insofar as a dominant paradigm of narrowed empiricism reigns, the distribution of knowledge into departments and specialties is only apparently but not really a reflection of the complexity and dimensionality of reality. The university may be a multiversity, but it appears to be moving more and more toward being a paradigmatic uniformity.

A second impoverishing effect of narrowed empiricism, equally serious, lies in another kind of suppression. Paradoxically, many of the specialty fields have supplanted an interest in the question of truth with a descriptive and phenomenalist interest in their subject matter.[26] There are, of course, many theories and interpretations of truth, but the competition between these is not the issue here. To be oriented to truth, whatever one's theory of truth, is to attend to the distinctive *claim* something presents to our perplexity and sense of mystery. A concern with truth characterizes all genuine sciences. Astronomy does not settle for descriptions and typologies of various cosmologies. It assesses each of the cosmologies it considers, using mathematical and other criteria. In many studies in the humanities and the social sciences, however, the assessment of truth is replaced with phenomenal description. A number of world religions are descriptively paraded before the student. The ancient and modern texts that confront the interpreter with all sorts of claims are translated and exegetically, contextually, and semiotically exposed without any attention's being paid to assessing the claims themselves. Masses of data about population trends, about poverty and crime, and about therapeutic techniques are gathered and analyzed without there being any assessment of the latent normative and evaluative aspects that make these things worth investigating. Literatures of the field from the past and present are summarized and monitored as if that were work on the subject itself. This is not to say that such descriptive, historical, typological, and statistical ventures have no value or cognitive outcome at all. There is a concern for the truth, or accuracy, of the description itself. What is marginalized and then suppressed is the claim behind the superficial claims of the data or texts, the claim posed by the situation itself or by the convictions manifest in the text. It is these deeper claims posed by moral issues, religious mythoi, societal alienation, and human pathology that are suppressed when the specialties in the humanities and the social sciences restrict themselves to the narrowed empiricist paradigm. Curiously, the scholar-teachers of these areas accept without question the normative, truth-oriented undertakings of the natural sciences at the same time that they renounce such undertakings in their own fields as improper advocacy.[27]

Both the suppression of dimensionality and the suppression of concern for truth have a corrupting effect on science and scholarship because they surrender science's paradoxical double-sidedness and the dialectic between two mutually corrective poles. At the one pole the scientist focuses on an abstracted subject matter. At the other pole the abstraction is corrected by reintroducing the subject's complexity, dimensionality, and relationality. When dimensionality and the concern for truth are suppressed, the scholar is content to pursue the abstraction, the focused research, without the correction that the synthetic pole introduces.

The Effects of Isolation

There are frequent complaints about the fragmented university, the multiversity that has lost its unity. The organization of the university into professional schools, disciplines, and departments is not usually what is being deplored, for the complexity of reality and the legitimacy of abstracting inquiry necessitate the distribution of cognitive and pedagogical tasks. Beyond this distribution, however, there is in today's university a distorting fragmentation promoted by large, competing "cultures" of athletics, administration, physical sciences, humanities, and medicine, each with its distinctive aims, special discourse, and power base. There is also the distorting fragmentation that owes to the smaller, professionalized specialty fields. How do the specialty fields fragment the university? How is it that the mutual isolation of the specialty fields must be considered one of the principal forms of the specialty fields' corruption of genuine science and the university?

It may not be immediately apparent that isolation is a constitutive condition of the specialty fields. As social entities the specialty fields exist in larger pedagogical areas and departments, and most specialty fields are in some sense interdisciplinary. The relationships between specialty fields in and between departments are, however, primarily political alliances, not cognitive interdependences, and the inter-disciplinary character of the specialty fields often lies mainly in adopting resources and procedural tools from other sciences to facilitate their own abstracting projects. Thus specialty fields employ mathematics, computer sciences, linguistics, ancient languages, logic, and the like. Specialization itself is, of course, an isolation, a cognitive residence in a closely defined categorical and methodological endeavor. A professionalized specialty field is isolated not only by the specializing focus but by the social reinforcement of the focus in the reward system and the specialty guild. But is there anything deleterious about this isolation, or about the constitution of the university by isolated research and teaching units? Isolated fields corrupt both the scholarship and the teaching of the university by condoning and even nurturing the anomaly of the uneducated scholar-teacher and the trivialization of scholarship.

It is not surprising that when specialists talk to one another about their specialties, they are not especially successful. The cognitive results of a specialty may or may not be communicable to a more general public. The route to the results (symbolic logic, higher mathematics, statistic analysis, linguistic analysis) usually is not. What is new in the university organized into specialty fields is that cross-specialist conversation cannot take for granted a general education as the larger frame of discourse. This is not to say that no larger framework of communication exists at all. Professors, like the majority of the population, are literate, read the newspapers, follow sports, watch television, vote in elections, purchase houses, and sometimes even go to church. The quotidian provides a background that conversing specialists, like anyone else, will draw on. But cross-specialty conversation cannot take for granted a participation on the part of the conversants in the multiplicity of paradigms represented in the university. The conversation cannot, in other words, take for granted a larger learning, a transcendence of the specialty field, that has some understanding of the complexity of reality and of alternative interpretive paradigms. The professor who embodies the larger learning, a privileged knowledge, is of a fast-vanishing breed. Therefore, the isolation of the specialty fields is first and foremost an isolation from learning itself, from a *paideia* that would enable the scholar to adopt a variety of cognitive and hermeneutical postures. Insofar as specialists have little awareness of the cognitive paradigms occurring in the larger learning and therefore are inclined to misprize the larger learning itself, they do not necessarily regret their isolation. The larger perspectives of learning suggest to the specialist the reward system's most dreaded types, the generalist and the dilettante.[28]

But the specialty fields are not isolated just from the larger learning. It may sound astonishing to say that specialists are isolated also from their very own discipline and teaching area. Nonetheless it is true, and in fact disciplines may not survive in the modern university. In their place are teaching areas whose social unit is the department. These teaching areas are merely administrative jurisdictions inhabited by specialists. The identity and labor of the specialists are less defined by disciplines (psychology, sociology, American literature) than they are by the social network and agenda of the specialty, by the professional association and the invisible college. The graduate program associated with a specialty field more than likely does not require an education in the discipline itself but focuses on a branch or subdiscipline and finally on a specialized area of research. The consequence is that cross-specialty conversations within common teaching areas not only cannot presuppose a framework of larger learning but cannot even presuppose the framework of the specialty's own discipline.

What is the harm in this isolation? When a specialty does its work in isolation from the diverse postures and paradigms of learning, it loses most of the resources by which it can correct its own abstraction. It is in the world of the larger learning that one confronts the complexity, mystery, and dimensionality of reality. For this, more is needed than simply a consultation with another specialty. There must be a constant correction of one's focused specialty, a restoring of the abstracted subject matter to its concreteness and contextuality. The specialty field by itself makes no such correction, content as it is with the progress it makes in its selected paradigm and reinforced as it is by the rewards of its social environment. When a specialty field's connection with its discipline is reduced to being a matter of political alliances, the specialty suffers because it is cut off from resources in the discipline which would correct its abstraction. In addition, the discipline itself suffers. The discipline falls into the background and may even disappear as the teaching area becomes a mere aggregate of specialty projects.[29] The discipline is by its very nature based in a science and thus exists only as some type or genre of things evokes a successful cognitive response. Biology can be a genuine discipline—and science—only because there are living things. Economics can be a genuine science only where human beings produce economies. The phenomena themselves create and preside over the science, and thus there must be a constant struggle with what these phenomena are, with their complexity, contextuality, dimensionality, and relations to other things. It is just this struggle that the specialty fields do not engage in, for the reason that this is a *disciplinary* struggle and they have only minimal contact with the discipline.[30] Because of specialization the subject matter of disciplines is no longer thematized as such. The subject matters of sociology, psychology, religion, philosophy, economics, English, history are viewed not as realities but as aggregates of what the technical methods research.[31]

The second major effect of the enduring isolation of the specialty field is trivialization.[32] The specialty field is already narrowly focused. Because it is narrowly defined, the horizon of its advance is internal, with the focus on increasingly detailed problems of a tiny cognitive territory. The movement of inquiry is toward problems of decreasing significance, problems that are further and further removed from the discipline and from the reality thematized by the discipline. The specialist may come to know more than anyone else in the world about something, but the knowledge is so discrete and refined, it has little import.[33] In disciplines whose subject matter is more or less fixed—for example, an ancient text—and in disciplines where there has been a surfeit of investigation, there is still a moving horizon of inquiry, but the focus is always on new methods to interpret that more or less fixed material. A book of an ancient canon or a famous literary figure from the past can be psychoanalyzed, deconstructed, psychohistoricized, structuralized, and phenomenologized. But the neomethodologies give scope only to a kind of artificial ingenuity whose subtleties grow more implausible with each new analysis.

The situation is different in sciences whose investigations are directed toward ever-changing social situations, sciences such as agroeconomics. They will never be trivialized by a surfeited research as long as their subject matter continues to change. But even here the discipline itself is pushed into the background by the technological orientation of the research. One cannot help wondering whether the university's cognitive endeavors should not have a different character from that of the research done in, by, and for government and industry.

The prospect is dim that the present state of affairs in the university will change in the near future. In the nature of the case, the specialty fields are insulated from the only resources that might correct their selected abstractions and complement their favored methods. The specialty fields are in this way deprived of any external horizon of development. They become enclaves nicely protected from criticism beyond themselves.[34] Furthermore, both the external support systems created by their professionalization and the reward system of the university help to hold them in place.[35] The specialty sciences of applied research will of course go where the action is. But there is little promise in that of fundamental correction. It is particularly dispiriting that the worst corruption of the university's historical aims is found not in marginal schools but in those that international consensus considers the best. Ironically, the more determined a university is to improve its reputation and its contributions to scholarship and teaching, the more warmly hospitable it is to the professionalized specialty fields. Once again the "best and the brightest" may be the makers and shapers of the worst.

NOTES

1. Jaroslav Pelikan quotes William Clyde DeVane, at one time the dean of Yale College, as saying that "90 percent of the new doctors of philosophy would enter the teaching profession, [and] that once their dissertations were accepted, most of them would never undertake further research" (*Scholarship and Its Survival: Questions on the Idea of Graduate Education* [Princeton: Carnegie Foundation for the Advancement of Teaching, 1983], 9).

2. No one doubts that the university is, in fact, fragmented. This fragmentation is not simply a cognitive disunity but a splintering into very large social entities of power and influence. I see not the "two cultures" of C. P. Snow but five cultures whose varying degrees of autonomy depend on their ability to generate their own financial base. They include the university's administrative complex, the medical complex, the athletic complex, the sciences (whose base funding is significantly outside the university), and the humanities (whose legitimacy and presence depend more on the internal values and good will of the university and less on the ability to generate independent funding). Each of these five cultures has its own aims, ethos, and even characteristic discourse.

3. To define sciences as problem-solving undertakings is insufficient. Almost every aspect of a business involves problem solving in some sense. A science results from applying appropriate cognitive methods to an abstracted *type* or *genre* of reality: life, human being, the human past, formal structures. Most of the schemes for classifying sciences, including the one proposed by Rudolf Carnap, presuppose that the discreteness of each science is created by the type of reality to which it is directed. Carnap's scheme is found in the *International Encyclopedia of Unified Sciences,* ed. Otto Neurath et al., and published as a two-volume work under the title *Foundations of the Unity of Science* (Chicago: Univ. of Chicago Press, 1955–70). Carnap's essay begins on p. 45 of vol. 1.

4. Ernest Nagel has a view of science broad enough to include history. In his view, what carries science beyond common-sense knowledge is the move to explanation, an employment of "explanatory principles" that can account for a puzzling diversity of phenomena (*The Structure of Science* [New York: Harcourt, Brace and World, 1961], 4).

5. This is a very truncated and even objectivist account of the tragic character of science. The focus of this account is on the requirements of the object or subject matter. A deeper violation occurs in the price the scientist pays for focusing. Not only are other aspects and relations in the complexity of the

object neglected but the cognitive situation itself is distorted by the subject-to-object formulation of the relation. To use the language of Heidegger, a focusing cognitive inquiry distorts both the very being-in-the-world of the individual scientist and the being-with of the scientific community.

6. James H. Bunn has explored the dimensional aspects of signs, tools, and models in the framework of semiotics. See his *The Dimensionality of Signs, Tools, and Models* (Bloomington: Indiana Univ. Press, 1981).

7. A lifelong project of Alfred Schutz was to work through the primary methodological dilemma handed on in the work of Max Weber. Schutz's project begins with his 1932 work *Der sinnhafte Aufbau der sozialen Welt*, translated in 1967 under the title *The Phenomenology of the Social World*. The problem, grasped clearly by Weber himself, is set forth in chap. 1 and concerns how an objectively oriented social science can do justice to a subject matter whose very essence is human acts of subjective meaning. See also Schutz, "On the Methodology of the Social Sciences," in *Collected Papers* (The Hague: Martinus Nijhoff, 1967), vol. 1. The problem posed by Weber and Schutz evinces a sense of the dimensional complexity of the social world.

8. For a history of the classification of sciences up to the end of the nineteenth century, see Robert Flint, *Philosophy as Scientia Scientiarum; and A History of Classifications of the Sciences* (Edinburgh and London: William Blackwood & Sons, 1904). In the twentieth century attempts to construct an architectonics of sciences are rare. One of the more impressive but now outdated attempts is by the philosopher-theologian Paul Tillich. See "Das System der Wissenschaften nach Gegenständen und Methoden" (1923), in *Gesammelte Werke*, vol. 1, *Frühe Hauptwerke* (Berlin: Evangelische Verlagsanstalt, 1959).

9. The character of science as occurring within social history is illuminated by recent well-known studies of science. These histories, sociologies, and philosophies of science approach science as a complex with a social history, a complex that forms dominant paradigms, draws on past tradition, and retains degrees of social power. See Thomas Kuhn, *The Structure of Scientific Revolutions*, 2d ed. (Chicago: Univ. of Chicago Press, 1970); Michel Foucault, *The Order of Things: An Archaeology of the Human Sciences* (New York: Random House, 1970); and Paul Feyerabend, *Against Method* (New York: Schocken Books, 1978).

10. The distinction between sciences and disciplines is not always acknowledged. Marc Belth's four criteria for a discipline pertain to what I am calling a science. According to him there is no necessary instructional aspect to a discipline (*Education as a Discipline: A Study of the Role of Models in Thinking* [Boston: Allyn and Bacon, 1965], 6–7). Similarly, John McIntyre argues that all disciplines require a given, models, and distinctive methods, but he says nothing about any distinction between disciplines and sciences (*The Shape of Christology* [Philadelphia: Westminster Press, 1966], 11). James Michael Lee does distinguish disciplines and sciences but only in the sense that disciplines

are smaller units of sciences (*The Shape of Religious Instruction* [Dayton: Pflaum Press, 1971], 95). In his view the discipline is the "smallest integral irreducible body of knowledge" and a science is a combination of disciplines. In my view, these interpretations pass over the distinction indicated both by the etymology of the two terms and by the existence of two different phenomena occurring in quite different contexts. For etymological differences, see the *Oxford English Dictionary*, s.v. "disciplines" and "sciences." For the distinctive instructional context of a discipline, see Joseph C. Kiger's essay, "Discipline," in *The Encyclopedia of Education*, ed. Lee C. Deighton (New York: Macmillan Co., 1971). Thomas Aquinas offers a distinction closely resembling that between disciplines and sciences when he argues that the seven liberal arts are not divisions of science, pertaining as they do to the initial stages of learning and constituting paths to the secrets of philosophy (*The Division and Method of the Sciences*, a translation of questions 5 and 6 of his commentary on the *De Trinitate* of Boethius [Institute of Medieval Studies, 1953]).

11. Although the distinction between sciences and disciplines is based primarily on the existence of two distinguishable undertakings that occur in different contexts, it is confirmed by the etymology of the terms. The English term "science" comes from the Latin *scientia*, which translates the Greek term *episteme*. Both terms mean the act, disposition, even accomplishment, of knowledge, and in a secondary usage, they also mean a special branch of knowledge. Instruction is not necessary to science in this sense. "Discipline," from *discere*, "to learn," does mean instruction and refers to the situation in which culture, knowledge, *paideia* are imported to learners.

12. Because of the irreducible differences between sciences, disciplines, and pedagogical areas, the task of organizing and classifying differs in each case. The "classification of sciences" is dominated by the diverse regions of reality that evoke research and scholarship. The organization of *pedagogical areas* results in a *curriculum* whose primary consideration is the age and situation of the students and the aims of the specific kind and level of educational environment (elementary, liberal-arts college, professional). The organization of *disciplines* will reflect but not be identical with the classification of sciences, simply because disciplines occur in a school and reflect the way in which the aims of the school come together with science and scholarship.

13. Richard Rorty, drawing on the "revolution in philosophy" typified in the work of John Dewey, Martin Heidegger, and Ludwig Wittgenstein, offers a strong criticism of traditional views of philosophy as a "science" whose subject matter is the timeless or ahistorical foundation of all knowledge (*Philosophy and the Mirror of Nature* [Princeton: Princeton Univ. Press, 1979]). In Rorty's view philosophy is less a distinctive method for arriving at truth and knowledge than a hermeneutic and edifying conversation.

14. The supplanting of classical education had begun centuries before. The

"battle of the books" as Swift described it in *The Tale of a Tub* concerned the threat posed to classical education by the new education.

15. See Burton J. Bledstein, *The Culture of Professionalism: The Middle Class and the Development of Higher Education in America* (New York: W. W. Norton & Co., 1976).

16. For a brief historical account of the professionalization of higher education, see Christopher Jencks and David Reisman, *The Academic Revolution* (Garden City, N.Y.: Doubleday & Co., 1968), chap. 1.

17. Bledstein, *Culture of Professionalism*, 327 n. 64.

18. See Diana Crane, *Invisible Colleges: Diffusion of Knowledge in Scientific Communities* (Chicago: Univ. of Chicago Press, 1972).

19. Ibid., 54.

20. Jencks and Reisman argue that American graduate programs have been slow to follow the lead of the sciences in cross-disciplinary collaboration (*Academic Revolution*, 523).

21. Alfred Schutz, *Reflections on the Problem of Relevance* (New Haven: Yale Univ. Press, 1970), 66–68.

22. The convergence of quantity, specialism, and the tenure time clock makes one suspect that some of the "slow-starting" great scholars and scientists of past generations would never have been awarded tenure at the "best," research-oriented universities. This is because these figures frequently spent the early years of their careers building very solid and broad foundations for their work, foundations necessary for seminal breakthroughs in a discipline. The scientist or scholar who occupies a specialty field from the very beginning never has sufficient time to become related to the larger learning or even to the discipline itself. Tillich, the most influential and best-known philosophical theologian from the 1940s to the 1960s, wrote two short doctoral theses in 1910 and 1912. From that time until 1924, when he was promoted to associate professor at the University of Marburg, he had published none of the major works that eventually established his reputation. A modern research-oriented university may or may not have regarded his "System der Wissenschaften" (1923) as sufficient evidence for promotion to tenure. During a twelve-year period, which was interrupted by a stint as chaplain in World War I, Tillich was building his own foundations, reading through the history of theology and philosophy, participating in political movements, working out the basic concepts on the nature of religion, the philosophy of religion, and religion and culture (politics), and reforging Schelling and the philosophy of identity, all of which made possible the astonishing accomplishments that began once Tillich was well into his forties.

23. Feyerabend addresses himself to what I am calling the paradigm of narrow empiricism in his account of sciences that see themselves as pure domains of research constituted by stable "facts" and that resist all insights which would blur their boundaries (*Against Method*, intro.).

24. Flint, writing in 1904, speaks of the "evil intellectual and moral influ-

ences of specialism" because of the tendency of specialists to devalue work other than their own and to make their own specialty the measure of the universe, thus missing the truths that lie between the sciences (*Philosophy as Scientia Scientiarum; and A History of Classifications of the Sciences*, 18, 24). Fifty years ago the Spanish philosopher José Ortega y Gasset devoted a chapter of his work *The Revolt of the Masses* (New York: W. W. Norton & Co., 1932) to the "barbarism of specialization." Comparing the ever-narrowing sciences to cells of a beehive, he describes the specialist as a learned ignoramus who has the attitudes of primitive, uneducated human beings on virtually everything but the specialty, a human being satisfied in his or her limitations. The harshest complaint may be that of Frederick Rudolph, the historian of higher education, who describes a "college professor digging up the upper skull and lower canine tooth of a Neanderthal man. It is a contrast between growth and petrification, the Neanderthal man representing growth . . ." (*The American College and University: A History* [New York: Alfred A. Knopf, 1962], 401).

25. Empiricism itself is not the issue here. Any genuine empiricism will attend to its subject matter in the specific and distinctive way that that subject matter is available to experience and cognition. Genuine empiricism is open to many paradigms of inquiry and knowledge. "Narrowed empiricism" as one of these paradigms is not problematic for subject matters, e.g., natural sciences, which are appropriate to it. It is a problem, first, in cognitive endeavors whose subject matter presses for other paradigms, and second, as a general ontology of reality and knowledge. The reason the paradigm of narrowed empiricism is an inadequate ontology is that it violates the founding principle of any ontology by making reality subject to method and not, as it should be, the reverse. By doing this, it identifies reality with the product of a methodological focusing or abstraction, and hence suppresses the concreteness, relationality, complexity, and horizonality of reality.

26. Calvin Schrag senses an abandonment of truth claims when sociology as sociologism forgets the "contents of culture" and social reality and focuses only on quantitative changes in the milieu (*Radical Reflection and the Origin of the Human Sciences* [West Lafayette, Ind.: Purdue Univ. Press, 1980], 1–2). Something similar occurs in psychology as psychologism, and in history as historicism.

27. For a criticism of the nonadvocacy and truth-neutral way of studying and teaching religion, see my "The Place of Theology in the Study of Religion," *Religious Studies and Theology* 5 (1986): 9–29.

28. The mind-set of the isolated specialty field is signaled by the territorial metaphors used to distinguish field from field. In the Middle Ages and through the nineteenth century the dominant metaphors for the divisions of the sciences were cosmological and biological. This accords with the purpose of the metaphors, namely, to show the relations of these regions of reality to one another and to the whole of reality. Thus we have the metaphor of heaven and its spheres (Dante), and of a tree and its branches (Bentham). The growth

stages of organic things also provided a metaphor for relating the sciences to one another (Kant, Hegel, Comte). One hears little of such metaphors now, for the reason that the classification of sciences is only rarely attempted. The traditional metaphors today tend to be displaced by political ones reflecting the view that the fields are territories. Imperialism thus becomes the primary academic transgression, the invasion of another's cognitive territory.

29. "A discipline is at bottom nothing more than an administrative category" (Jencks and Reisman, *Academic Revolution*, 523). See also David Reisman, *Constraint and Variety in American Education* (Lincoln: Univ. of Nebraska Press, 1956), 94; Reisman here describes the disciplines as veto groups.

30. The loss of connection with the discipline is signaled by the way specialty fields give an account of the "discipline" in which they fall. The question of the nature, scope, and subject matter of the discipline is entertained as a sociological question, answerable by a typology of the different specializations being undertaken. Thus the unifying subject matter of the discipline is identified with the social distribution of the specialty fields. The discipline, in other words, is seen as an aggregate of specialized undertakings.

31. I have used the term "reality" throughout this chap. It will not be a popular term for many readers. Phillip Rieff would probably say it is one of the "god-terms" now lost to a therapeutic and cultureless society (*Fellow-Teachers* [New York: Harper and Row, 1972], 39). One of the few explorations of the meaning of the term "reality" can be found in Herbert Spiegelberg's *Doing Phenomenology* (The Hague: Martinus Nijhoff, 1975), chap. 9.

32. Various recent authors have commented on the trivialization of the academy's scholarship. Rieff speaks of "masses of will-be glorified clerks, with Ph.D.'s" (*Fellow-Teachers*, 97). Bledstein argues that as research becomes more restricted, it is removed from public knowledge and public issues of the sort that relate to real social crisis: issues of race, power, injustice (*Culture of Professionalism*, 228–30). He holds that in this way professionalization is a taming of the university. "Cosmic questions" are eliminated as counterproductive to the reward system. Diana Crane argues that the reward system encourages quickly producible quantities of research that is of questionable value and it threatens those who are inclined to do research across and beyond their specialties (*Invisible Colleges*, 108–9).

33. "The difference between good scholarship and great scholarship is, as often as not, the general preparation of the scholar in fields other than the field of specialization" (Pelikan, *Scholarship and Its Survival*, 26).

34. For a description of how specialties function to isolate themselves from criticism, see Schrag, *Radical Reflection*, 3.

35. In Feyerabend's view the sciences are so frozen by rigid traditions that it will require a generation of "professional anarchists" to get them to push beyond their own boundaries (*Against Method*, intro. and chap. 16).

4

The Place of Theology
in the Study of
Religion

Our topic is the place of theology in the teaching of religion in colleges
and universities. The issue has been on the scene since World War II.[1]
What keeps it before us? I must confess a certain confusion and
vagueness about what has happened in the past decade in departments
and programs of religious studies across the country.[2] I do not possess
firm data on the criteria operative in faculty building, the presuppositions that inform the way the study of religion is parceled into areas of
expertise, or the general direction of change. But something about the
present situation permits or invites an inquiry about theology. Here I
can only surmise that a rather pervasive anomaly in religious studies is
responsible for the persistence of this issue. The anomaly is a conflict or
tension between certain conditions surrounding the origin of religious-
studies programs in this country and the character of the faculty
available to staff the programs. The creation of departments of religion
in colleges occurred primarily after the First World War and most of
the departments in state universities originated after the Second World
War.[3] These programs either replaced existing schools of religion
staffed by local clergy or filled a vacuum. In Europe, especially Germany, the faculty of theology was an integral part of the modern
university of the eighteenth-century Enlightenment, and although
certain theoretical issues eventually were raised about the propriety of
"theology" in the university, the possibility of religion as an area of
serious scholarship was never really questioned.[4] In the United States,
however, religious studies originated in a milieu of religious pluralism

An earlier version of this essay appeared in *Religious Studies and Theology* 5 (1985):
9–29.

that eschewed state support for any specific religious tradition. Hence, to gain its credentials in the academic community, it was imperative that religious studies purge itself of any religious parochialism and disengage itself from the prevailing expression of religion in this country—Christianity.

The other side of the anomaly is that the departments and programs of religious studies are heavily staffed with scholars educated in graduate programs whose legacy and specialties of scholarship are oriented to Western Christianity. The organization of areas of religious scholarship perpetuates the European theological encyclopedia of the faculty of theology.[5] One result of this anomaly is the continuing failure to propose a unifying subject matter of religious studies and a coherent rationale for divisions of labor. Another result is what might be called the conventional way of formulating the relation between theology and religious studies.

According to the conventional formulation, "religious studies" names an inclusive program or department that explores and teaches religion according to the canons of university scholarship.[6] Given these canons, no single religious faith can claim primacy or priority and religion itself must be interpreted without special pleading and under universal scholarly criteria. Theology, on the other hand, presupposes a specific religious community as its setting, a community that in the past has hindered and even persecuted university sciences. In addition, the educational institution accommodating theology is almost exclusively the professional school for clergy education. Furthermore, according to the conventional viewpoint, the grounds of validity and verification in theology are not publicly accessible but esoteric, private, and authoritarian. The code words for this apparent incompatibility of religious studies and theology are "objectivity" and "neutrality." Some of the literature of the 1950s and 1960s drew the lines this way and then argued that the university in its commitment to the autonomy of reason needed the radical monotheism of the Christian vision.[7]

It seems clear that the conventional view offers us only a pseudoproblem. There are no grounds, theoretically or historically, for refusing to teach specific historical religions, for instance, Buddhism or Judaism. Religious studies has done that all along. Hence the legitimacy of teaching any specific religious faith is not in question. Nor are there grounds, theoretically or historically, for affirming an incompatibility between advocacy and scholarship. No university would tolerate teachers of the nineteenth-century novel, of experimental psychology, of Marxist political science who were utterly neutral toward and utterly disengaged from their subject matter, who saw it as having no importance, as making no reality claims. The university assumes that the teacher-scholar is engaged with, affected by, and enthusiastic about the subject. For this reason not many modern universities would see D. T. Suzuki as unqualified to teach Buddhism because a Buddhist, or Karl Rahner as unqualified to teach Christianity because a Catholic priest. Accordingly, there have never been valid grounds stated for the excommunication of Christian studies from religious studies or of scholar-theologians who happen to be in some sense Christian believers. This is why any problem that arises from a supposed incompatibility between theology and religious studies is a pseudoproblem. Both advocacy and historical specificity are well-entrenched principles of university teaching.[8]

The conventional way of formulating the problem of relating theology and religious studies is part of our history. Given the recent influence of neo-orthodox theologies, and the need to obtain academic credentials for the study of religion, it does not surprise us. At the same time the controlling element in this conventional view is the politics of religious studies, the conditions to be met to obtain entrance into the university. Accordingly, I have expounded the conventional view of the problem only to lay it to rest and to proceed to another and much broader inquiry.

This broader inquiry approaches the problem of the place of theology in religious studies primarily as a problem of what it means to teach religion in the university. If that can only be determined, the contribution, irrelevance, or compatibility of "theology" to or with religious studies may become apparent. Since one's idea of the place of the teaching of religion in the university depends in part on one's analysis of the aims, trends, and problems of the modern university, the analysis will begin with a brief depiction of current university education. It will then consider the nature of religion itself and the nature of theology, especially in relation to its frequent caricatures. It will proceed to a consideration of the teaching of religion in the university, and finally, of the role of theology in the teaching of religion.

Technomania and the Academy

I shall not use the hackneyed term "crisis" to describe the present situation in higher education. If the term is usable at all, it would be to describe what is *needed* in higher education. Crisis at least suggests impending and possibly redemptive change. The larger society may or may not be in a crisis. But it does seem to be on the threshold of a cultural dark ages, of being caught in a trap it has set for itself.[9] Villains are frequently nominated: the international nation-state system, the consumer culture as correlate of the modern multinational corporation, world population growth out of control. Whatever the culprit, powerful and pervasive historical forces have generated not only new technologies on which most societies now depend but a new technological mentality. In the past, culture watchers have complained of the dominance of scientific paradigms and their impoverishing effect on education and culture. But the technological mentality must be distinguished from science. If science reflects passion for knowledge—the desire to understand—the technological mentality is the opposite of science, since its thrust is toward the ordering of corporate life. The result is that reality comes to mean data, and data mean quantified information pertinent to the ordering (controlling, recording, defending, storing, organizing, interpreting) of corporate life. Such are the society and age to which the university must justify its existence and from which it must draw its support.

Anyone who has to do with the modern university knows that its basic degree program may not yield an educated person. The university is described as a multiversity without unity or overall aim. Or it is said to divide into two cultures—science and the humanities—with little relation between them. (Three cultures might be more accurate if athletics are included.) If an educated person is only rarely the product of the modern university, this may have something to do with the way the university reflects the general societal identification of reality with data. The technological mind-set is widespread in the university, not in the sense that the faculty members think of themselves as technicians but rather that their model for scholarship is a discipline or science whose credentials and criteria are quantifiability and objectification. Thus we have data-oriented research and teaching setting the criteria of scholarship for the social sciences and establishing subtle paradigms of interpretation in history, philosophy, literature, and so forth. I do not want to exaggerate this, to belabor it to the point that the university is depicted as possessing a single milieu. It is simply that educated persons appear only rarely to come out of the university's basic degree program, and the main reason appears to be the dominance of the technological mind-set as a paradigm of scholarship and teaching.

What do we mean by an educated person? I can offer only some brief suggestions as to what we might mean—what a modern version of Greek *paideia* might be. Consider the following five marks. (1) An educated person is sufficiently exposed to a plurality of experiences and modes of interpretation to be self-conscious in his or her responses, decisions, and policies. (2) This self-consciousness has a critical dimension. It is a self-consciousness about evidence and what constitutes the establishment of a claim or the grounding of a tradition or policy. (3) This critical attitude reflects the capacity to look behind things and beneath things, to respond not just to surfaces and face values. Looking beneath is characteristic of the Freudian hermeneutical revolution, as applied to the individual, and the Marxist hermeneutic, as applied to the corporate. (4) The educated person is self-conscious in his or her general existence in society, in the exercise of discerned obligation. In other words, the person knows enough about the workings of local and larger societies to interpret critically issues of social praxis. (5) The educated person is sufficiently introduced to the heritage of cultural accomplishments (say, in literature, music, the arts) to enjoy aesthetic dimensions of experience beyond those which are commercially and faddishly orchestrated. This is the hedonistic, aesthetic dimension of education. In other words, the total impact of the various types of knowledge and modes of thinking which occur in university education has experiential, pluralistic, hermeneutic, critical, rational, political, and aesthetic dimensions. The educated person is thus shaped a certain way, and this shaping is not simply the production of capacities of technical functioning but the evoking of ways of existing in and interpreting reality. I realize the tentativeness of such a list. I offer it only to illustrate a serious point: that education in its most genuine sense has to do with capacities of responding to and interpreting the complexities, the various dimensions, of reality. The university's current drift toward a data-oriented mind-set and its failure to educate can be turned about only by a new hermeneutic self-consciousness. That is to say, the university needs broader, more flexible paradigms of interpretation if it is to be an occasion and environment of genuine education.

Dimensions of Religiousness

Since our exploration concerns religious studies and theology, the frequently posed question of the nature of religion is unavoidable. There are those who would set to rest both that question and the term "religion."[10] Sympathetic as I am to that view, I fear that the loss of a unifying term, "religion," would simply turn the whole discussion over to the data-oriented mind-set and the view that "religion" does not exist but data about religious behavior do. The value of Wilfred Cantwell Smith's warning lies in its criticism of religion as a kind of reified historical entity behind other reified historical entities like Christianity or Judaism. The issue posed here is the genre question. What *sort* of thing is religion? It seems apparent, first of all, that religion is not a region or entity but an aspect of human, historical, and personal processes, events, and relations. The grasp of this aspect calls for a complex and flexible posture of interpretation which includes, among other things, philosophical scrutiny of the strangeness of the human being and its experience of the world, as well as a probing of the complex strata of human language. One of the better succinct definitions of religion occurs in an essay of the late Arthur McGill. According to him, religion is the "human response to those superior powers from which man [sic] sees himself and his communities deriving life and death."[11] This definition has several advantages. First, it articulates the sense in which religion poses the issue of the nature of the most comprehensive context of human existence, without specifying that context theistically. Second, the concept of human response leaves room for both personal or individual and social or corporate dimensions of response. Thus, Smith's proposal to replace "religion" with the two themes of personal religiousness and corporate tradition reflects the two dimensions of this human response.

My own reformulation of the definition would go something like this. The personal-individual aspect of religion (of religiousness) originates in the strange way in which the human being is self-conscious about its own deepest problem and situatedness. The human being exists in the world not in the mode of utter unreflective contentment, indifference, or instinctuality but in self-conscious anxiety about the meaning of its experience and destiny. Its most fundamental striving or desires (for knowledge, meaning, security, happiness, contentment) move past or through its worldly environment and thus occur on an infinite horizon.[12] When the human being responds to what it construes that infinite horizon to be (God, Atman, nature, being, sacred powers), this anthropological structure generates religiousness or piety. The institutional-corporate aspect of religion originates concomitantly with the personal-individual aspect since the construal of the nature of the infinite horizon always occurs in connection with language, symbols, myths, processes of traditioning which preserve these things, rituals that enact them, and so forth. If we are in any way close to characterizing religion here, we can conclude that religion does pose a real issue, that is to say, an issue of truth and reality. This issue is simply the character of whatever constitutes, empowers, orders, founds, or even assaults the comprehensive environment (world) of the human being.

On the basis of this outrageously brief analysis I identify three aspects or dimensions of religion that are so constitutive and pervasive that to ignore any one of them would be to distort seriously the interpretation of religion. The first aspect is that about which religion itself is serious, that which grounds its seriousness, namely, its concern with truth and reality. This is the aspect of the ultimate horizon of human existence. We can call it the aspect of transcendence. Religion's second aspect is its presence in individual human experience. Religion expresses a distinctive way in which the human being is a human being, copes with a dangerous environment, and strives for the meaning of things. Presupposed here are certain ways that the human being is temporal and spatial, linguistic and intersubjective. Expressed here are ways the human being experiences itself as problematic, vulnerable, dangerous, and evil. This could be called the anthropological dimension of religion. Because of it, religiousness concerns not only the human being's most comprehensive environment but its deepest and most comprehensive problematic.[13] The third aspect of religion is the corporate and the institutional. This is the social and cultural sedimentation of religious experience which creates continuity over time and enables religion to take the form of complex historical movements. Here we are dealing with religion as a social continuity, a traditioning, an institutionality.

These three aspects or dimensions presuppose, of course, a genre decision and definition of religion. They also indicate three requirements or criteria for any adequate study of religion. In sum, they say that religion poses a distinctive truth or reality issue, is a distinctive dimension of human experience, and is culturally specific and concrete. This dimensional complexity is what opens religion to a variety of methods in the social sciences and humanities. The same complexity also poses a subject matter for a focused exploration whose results would remain hidden if the study of religion occurred only in a variety of separate sciences. Because of its dimensional distribution, this subject matter is not identical with simply the phenomenal, historical manifestation of religion in texts, corporate activities, artifacts, and the like. For part of the subject matter is that which makes the text important, that is, certain claimed insights into or about a human being in relationship to its most comprehensive horizon and in its deepest problematic.

Theology: Toward a Working Definition

What is theology? The question has been so often posed that one hesitates to raise it again, on risk of boring the audience to death. Yet, this essay is about theology, so a detour around the question is not possible. Like most terms with a long history and multiple usages, "theology" both calls forth caricatures and harbors ambiguities. According to the caricatures, theology is the systematic rendition of Scripture, a Christian gnosis whose units are doctrines, a precritical apologetic for beliefs established by church authority, the content of an established system of beliefs, or a now discredited "metaphysical" mode of objectifying thought. The most serious problem is posed by the ambiguities harbored, because these ambiguities are ambiguities of genre, ambiguities concerning the kind of thing theology is. The term "theology" is itself, as is well known, pre-Christian, occurring in Plato and Aristotle, but it was quickly co-opted by the Christian community as a term for the knowledge or understanding of God and the things of God attending redemption and revelation. With the rise of the universities in Europe, it began to take on connotations of a discipline, that is, of knowledge that had a self-conscious basis in demonstration, knowledge made aware of itself by awareness of its ground. With the rise of the modern university in eighteenth-century Europe, this one knowledge and discipline began to splinter. The Enlightenment produced a number of quasi-independent sciences in the theological faculty (Bible, church history, moral theology, dogmatics). Once this happened, the term "theology" became a cluster term for a faculty, a set of disciplines, dogmatic theology.[14] In addition, the term is sometimes expanded to mean any reflective-interpretive enterprise of a specific religious faith, in which case there are Hindu theology, Jewish theology, and so forth.

Given these historical drifts of meaning, what "theology" are we attempting to relate to religious studies? In my view the expansion of the meaning of theology to include interpretive undertakings occurring in the major religious faiths is more or less a permanent historical occurrence. It may be the case that in earlier times theology named a distinctively Christian enterprise. Now, however, it appears that all major world religions have a self-consciousness that prompts some of their representatives both to criticize and sift their tradition and to articulate it apologetically in relation to modernity. This expansion prevents us from identifying theology with the self-conscious reflection of any one religion, but it does not yet say what it is.

The only thing I can do here is present my own conception of theology in the hope of striking some familiar chords. I begin with a definition. *Theology is the reflectively procured insight and understanding which encounter with a specific religious faith evokes*.[15] Note the elements of the definition. First, it presupposes the historically incarnated or determinate character of religious faith. Religion occurs in the concreteness of history and culture. Even if there is an understanding evoked by considering major historical religious faiths in their interrelations, the understanding does not seem to have a theological character. Second, understanding is the sort of thing theology itself is. Accordingly, theology is primarily an understanding and only secondarily a science or discipline. Although I do not want to deny that theology can be a scholarly discipline, I see that as one of several levels or forms which understanding might reach. This being the case, theological understanding occurs in human beings who reflectively encounter a specific religious faith. Hence, it is not restricted to the professional leadership of that faith (the ministry, the priesthood, the rabbinate) nor to the academic leadership. Even if the leaders have distinctive theological responsibilities, they have no monopolistic possession of theological understanding. Third, theology occurs in a reflective mode. It is not simply the spontaneous insightfulness that may be generated by participation in or encounter with a specific faith. Theological understanding is *considered* understanding. It occurs to some degree as self-conscious understanding and hence has a deliberative, purposive character. The theologically disposed person does what is appropriate to the specificity of the religious faith in order to gain insight. Let me repeat that the understanding in question is directed to the threefold complexity of the religious faith, not simply to its phenomenal facticity, its manifestness.

Finally, that which evokes the understanding is encounter with the faith. I put it this way to avoid making belief-ful participation in the community of faith the prerequisite of theological understanding. Probably most theological understanding in fact occurs in the context of belief. But it seems to me that the issue itself is something of a trap. To ask whether theological understanding is available to the so-called nonbeliever is to pose an unanswerable question. On what grounds does one human being tell another that he or she is incapable of understanding or insight? If it is neither possible nor desirable to describe conditions and list credentials for understanding the metaphysical poets or Goethe's *Faust*, why should we attempt to do this for the reflective understanding of the Tao te Ching or the Letter to the Romans? Probably there are different types of understanding evoked by Buddhist, Jewish, Islamic, and Christian faith. Acknowledging that does not appear to entail the limitation of theological understanding to belief-ful cultic participation.

Hermeneutic Principles in the Study of Religion

What does it mean to teach religion in the university? My exploration of this theme will portray an ideal situation, not one that is actual. At the level of actuality, no clear and coherent answer to the question has won a consensus. "Religious studies," we remind ourselves, does not name a solution to this question. It is an alternative designation for departments of religion, and therefore names a program of studies, not a discipline, science, or even philosophy of the teaching of religion. Because it does name a department or program, it implies some unity of approach, perhaps even a subject matter; hence religious studies is distinguished from the "study of religion," which is distributed among the various sciences of the university.[16] Accordingly, some way is sought to justify this unified pedagogy and area of scholarship. The existence of a program or department of religious studies raises the issue of whether there is a subject matter correlative to the department or faculty which would be distorted by distribution among various disciplines.

I venture that the subject matter of religious studies is religion, as this has already been described. Religion, it will be recalled, is not an entity or a field of entities but an aspect of human experience which has specific historical and cultural expressions. Religion as religiousness is the individual human being's response to what it discerns to be the most comprehensive powers of its environment. Religion as historical tradition is the corporate and symbolic expression of that discernment rendered into forms of repetition, transmission, institution. If this is what religion is, what does it mean to teach it and investigate it?

I begin with what appears to be self-evident. To teach and study religion in the university is to apply the canons of universal scholarship to religion. "Canons of universal scholarship" sounds innocent enough, but we recall that the university is not inoculated against the powerful and prevailing cultural tendency to reduce reality to data—against, that is, the technological mind-set. Hence, "canons of scholarship" can refer to a very specific paradigm of knowledge, inquiry, and method. We are all familiar with the outrageous distortions that any field can perpetrate under the name of scholarship. Scholarship, science, *Wissenschaftlichkeit* are valid aims for the university in the study of religion. But any appropriation of those aims must be critical of unsuitable paradigms and insistent that it is religion itself that is being studied.[17] If religion does constitute a claim about reality, if it presupposes and shapes human experience, and if it is perpetually embodied in social forms, the scholarly study of religion will involve a struggle with those dimensions. It needs to be scholarship attended by a strong hermeneutic self-consciousness.[18] What then would be some of the features of a hermeneutic of religion?

Since the object or subject matter of a study determines method, and not vice versa, the hermeneutic principles for the study of religion are subject to the nature of religion itself.[19] I have described religion as making a reality claim concerning the widest context of experience, as presupposing and shaping human experience in distinctive ways, and as socially and historically concrete. These features undergird three hermeneutic principles for the study and teaching of religion: principles of concreteness, experientiality, and reality.

The principle of concreteness protects the historical integrity of religion. It serves as a caution sign against subjecting one religion to the canons of another and against translating religion into "religion in general" or into some wider genus (morality, aesthetics, primitive science). The actuality of religion is a historical and social actuality, and this invariably includes particular origins, traditions, modes of social duration, myths, primary symbols, ritual activities, and institutions. Grasping a specific religious faith sets further distinctive hermeneutic requirements to which the student of religion must attend.

Second, the principle of experientiality requires the student to attend to the distinctive way religion presupposes and illumines human being in the world. Does religion, for instance, presuppose the distinctive way in which human beings exist in an imperiling world in the mode of anxiety? Does it assume human temporality and the orientation to the future? Does it not only presuppose these things but reshape them, affect them in some way? Is the fundamental way a religion construes the most comprehensive environment of the human being closely connected to a paradigm of the human problem, a paradigm of suffering or moral evil or finite ignorance? Is there a distinctive kind of experiencing or intentionality called forth by sacred power? All these questions address the experiential dimension and call for the kinds of inquiry that can illumine it: psychological, ontological, existential, intersubjective. Furthermore, if this dimension is totally passed over, religion itself remains hidden. The symbols, rituals, institutions, and the like that are its historically concrete side become just external data.

Third, the principle of reality asks the student of religion to take religion's own claims seriously. I previously argued that religion's claims tend to find their unity in the issue of the most comprehensive environment or powers before which human life is conducted. The anthropological correlate of this is the human problem in its most comprehensive, most pervasive, most radical sense: the human problem as encompassing suffering, evil, hubris, and illusion. The correlation between the comprehensive human problem and the ultimate environment of that problem poses reality questions. Nor does the reality issue go away, as traditional positivism assumes, with modern scientific paradigms of reality and knowledge. It is rather that the quasi-religious character of those paradigms is exposed insofar as the paradigms pretend to be themselves the exhaustive account of the most comprehensive problem and environment of the human being.

There are subjects that find their way into teaching and study not because of their intrinsic worth or reality claims but because they are simply part of history and culture. Psychologists and sociologists will study the flat-earth society—not because of its cosmology but because it is an unusual and marginal cultural curiosity. Without the reality principle, religion (or a specific religion) becomes just that, a cultural curiosity. We study it because, like phrenology, astrology, and heavy-metal music, it is part of human culture. But the claims religion makes, the issues it poses, are not of the same order as the claims of these examples, that is, relatively straightforward empirical claims that can and should be qualified, tested, revised, and displaced. Since religion has to do with the most comprehensive setting of human life and being, in correlation with the most comprehensive form of the human problem, its issues do not disappear or reappear with new empirical discoveries. The issues, of course, have a history, and the varying opinions about the importance of the issues also have a history. Further, any expression of the issues is revisable and open to criticism. Nonetheless, the issues posed by religions attend the human way of experiencing the world. Hence, to reduce them to a cultural curiosity is to miss the phenomenon itself. Accordingly, without the third hermeneutic principle, the study of religion would become data-oriented scholarship, a distribution among a plurality of sciences, or some reductionistic theory indifferent to religion's self-manifestation. .

These hermeneutic principles do not constitute a specific method, one, for instance, designed to interpret religious texts. They describe what might be called the hermeneutic posture that religion evokes. The advantage of approaching religious studies by way of the three principles is that it does not require the study of religion to arrive at some sort of consensus about a religion behind the religions. Except as an identifiable aspect of human existence, a way of responding to a mysterious and imperiling environment, there is no such religion. Religious studies does not depend on a consensus about general religion in order to ground its scholarship or provide it with a subject matter. This situation is not unique in the university. No general theoretical consensus pertaining to human psyche, behavior, sociality, aesthetics, or economics grounds the enterprises of psychology, sociology, philosophy, and the like.

Another clarification: The hermeneutic posture called forth by religion is not an exception in the university but is an instance of a posture needed in almost every area of study in the university. Counterparts to the principles of concreteness, experientiality, and reality are important for any subject of serious study. The principle of concreteness seems to have a firm place in the university since the rigor of scholarship tends to be defined as proper methodological attention to detail, evidence, argument, and assumption. Such is the legacy of the post-Renaissance and Enlightenment historical consciousness. Yet something is clearly missing if study and teaching stop here. Sophocles' *Antigone*, the religous art of the Italian Renaissance, the French Revolution, the hermeneutic revolutions of both Marx and Freud, and seventeenth-century metaphysical poetry all proffer claims of a sort. Serious response to any of these is not response to a mere curiosity. To reduce them to curiosities, to suspend the reality question, can only trivialize them. Not only do they release their own kinds of claims upon us, they involve dimensions and depths of human experience. They pose issues of the character of aesthetic experience, historical knowledge, and moral decision. It is just those dimensions of science and education which are threatened by the data-oriented, technological mind-set. The point, however, is that when religious studies is fulfilling its scholarly and pedagogical responsibility under the guidance of its hermeneutic principles, it is furthering, not compromising, the principles important to a modern university.

The Common Plight of Religious Studies and Theological Studies

According to the conventional formulation of the relation between theology and religious studies, what produces the problem in the relation is theology's subjection to a specific religion. In contrast, religious studies by itself is presumed to be relatively unproblematic. Its credentials are established and its aims are clear. Assumed by the conventional view are the health and clarity of the university's condition, the sharing in this health and clarity by religious studies, and the incompatibility of the aims of theology with those of the university and of religious studies. The major problem with this conventional view is that it obscures the way in which general trends in Western culture and in the university have created problems for religious studies and theology alike. If there is a structural incompatibility, it is not between religious studies and theology but between the hermeneutic principles both of them require and the data-oriented methodological commitments and disciplinary loyalties of the university. Earlier I described the technological mind-set of contemporary Western society. Symptoms of this mind-set in the university are the failure of the university to formulate education as a *paideia*, an ideal of the educated person, and the trivialization and obscuring of subject matters because of a technical expository focus on discrete units of cognition (texts, events, causes, trends). In other words, the object of knowledge is assumed to be the phenomenal or surface entities that mediate data or are translatable into data.

One effect of this is the primacy and dominance of methodologically defined "scholarly disciplines" or sciences. The discipline is defined by its methodology, and the methodology controls and restricts teaching and inquiry. The primary commitment is, therefore, to the method—and the discipline—so that the object of knowledge cannot then set its own requirements for what is appropriate to understanding it. Given such primacy of method and discipline, the teacher and student tend to restrict their relation to the subject matter to technical, phenomenal exposition, and thus they are prevented from participation in the claim it makes on them and from really being affected by it. This is the general milieu in which both religious studies and theological studies must justify themselves and make their way.

Theology began to feel the effects of the data-oriented mind-set with the rise of the so-called modern university of Europe. The gains were obvious. Various aspects of corporate religious life (history, texts, events) could be studied in discrete, critical disciplines that were not subject to institutional or textual authorities. But the gains were accompanied by certain losses. One of the losses was theology itself, in the sense of a knowledge or understanding evoked by the claims set by texts and symbols. Theology became largely a matter of a professional school, an education pertinent to the priestly or ministerial leadership of churches. In clergy schools, theology was divided into disciplines, each with its method, literature, and guild loyalty. Existing primarily in independent disciplines, theological studies today reflect the problem of higher education in general. The primacy of method and of the independent discipline removes the obligation to teach religion or theology as reflectively procured understanding that encounters with a specific religious faith and is evoked by it. What is taught are the external units (language, texts) that scholarship can deal with, along with methodologies defining that scholarship. When these clergy-school disciplines do find their way into the university, their responsibility is neither religion nor theology but the mediation of the graduate-school specialties: American religion, Western Christian thought, early Christian literature, Old Testament.

It would be misleading to say that religious studies underwent the same historical development. Theology (theological understanding) underwent a splintering into disciplines, but there never was "religion" in the sense of some unitary type of understanding that later became splintered. Instead, religious studies was formed as a program of studies by joining together several graduate-school specialties in Christian studies and world religions. In religious studies there is not a ready subject but the search for a subject. Because of the dominance of methods and disciplines, the search has been directed not toward religion as an aspect of human existence but toward formally similar structures that generate comparative and typological undertakings. As with theological studies, the discipline orientation of religious studies has included important gains—for instance, widespread scholarly expertise in specific world religions. And like theological studies, religious studies participates in the general poverty of interpretation so widespread in the university. To gain its credentials, religious studies has had to assure a suspicious university community that it is capable of objective scholarly work employing data-oriented styles and methods, which suspend the hermeneutic principles of experientiality and reality.

In sum, theological studies and religious studies reflect the university's general eschewal of *paideia* and interpretation. This means that they both tend to give primacy to the discipline and make the requirements of the subject secondary. They both slip past the subject, instead mounting self-contained scholarly enterprises. The specific disciplines within them tend to avoid language and interpretive categories that might obscure disciplinary boundaries or compromise loyalty to their methods. Thus they contribute to the general resistance to a hermeneutic of experience and reality, which in turn limits scholarship to expounding and rehabilitating the unit of scholarly knowledge. Religious studies and theology, therefore, misread the situation when they identify each other as incompatibles. Such a reading obscures the larger forces that are preventing both of them from exploring what religion itself sets as reality claims and the dimensions of experience.

Religious Studies: Aims, Disciplines, and Postures

We cannot take up our final question—that of the place of theology and theological studies in religious studies—apart from a more specific consideration of what religious studies itself is. Two general rules pertinent to this question have emerged in the argument. The negative one is that there is no religion behind the religions. This means that there is neither an actuality nor an ideality that is an entity, an essence, a universal structure, an archetype, to be the referent of the term "religion." If this is the case, there is no object of religious scholarship and teaching in any of these senses. The positive general rule is a hermeneutic one and was set forth in the three principles of concreteness, experientiality, and reality. If there is, in fact, no religion behind the religions, what is it that offers itself for study? Certainly specific historical religions invite study and understanding, which would include both historical discernment of what constitutes the religions and consideration of what about them makes a reality claim. Specific historical religions manifest particular postures toward human existence and also certain formal, structural similarities; both the postures and the similarities offer themselves for exploration.

We are thus provided a clue to the *aims* of religious studies. A first aim is to explore and teach specific historical religions, both at the level of knowledge about them and at the level of encounter with the claims they set, the insights they proffer. A second aim is to explore and teach the structural similarities of historical religions. And a third aim is to attempt to illumine religiousness itself, religion as an aspect of human existence.

If religion is in fact the sort of object suggested here and if it does set these general aims in teaching and study, then certain hermeneutic postures are indicated. I am not talking about a specific hermeneutic theory but rather about the general principles of concreteness, reality, and experientiality. The three together protect the integrity, distinctiveness, and seriousness of religion.

I am in no position to suggest how religious studies might in fact embody fields of expertise. Given the aims and hermeneutic principles of religious studies, one thing seems inevitable. Because religiousness exists embodied in specific cultural and historical forms, religious studies inevitably involves scholarly and critical study of specific religious faiths, attempting to do full justice to each one's integrity and uniqueness. We must expect, then, that fields of expertise in religious studies will continue to include scholarly specialties coinciding with the divisions among the major religious faiths. Specialties that coincide with major faiths are, as we know, easily corruptible. Three ways in which scholarly specialties can be pursued so as to undercut the aims of religious studies are especially noteworthy.

First, the specialty can adopt the trappings of scholarship while practicing an advocacy that is uncritical, unhistorical, or obscurantist. The scholarship can serve as a thin veneer for an unhistorical absolutizing of the specific religious tradition. Presumably this is a rare but not unknown occurrence in modern universities.

Second, the scholarship of a specific historical religion can become itself so fragmented into independent disciplines that the individual teacher loses connection with the overall historical phenomenon.[20]

Third, the scholarly discipline and its method can be embraced without there also being embraced the requisite hermeneutic principles needed by the university and the field of study. Here the teacher loses the ability to use his or her scholarship to explore and test that which makes the whole undertaking important: the reality claims constituted by the religious faith. Hence, every scholar-teacher has some obligation to teach religion so that its concreteness is respected, its experiential dimension uncovered, and its reality claims, its potential insights, tested. Any teacher of religion needs both tools that enable scholarly expertise and tools that are pertinent to a hermeneutic oriented to understanding. Without both sets of tools, religion will be taught not as a dimension of human existence but as a collection of relatively independent clusters of historical data.

The Contribution of a
Theological Hermeneutic

We turn finally to the question of the role of theology in the study of religion which occurs in the university. According to the conventional formulation of the problem, theology's base in an actual religious community compromises its objectivity and its capacity to advance the critical and scholarly aims of the university. This essay has attempted another formulation of the problem, which breaks down into five steps: (1) Insofar as the present climate of the university is that of data-oriented scholarship, the "canons of university scholarship" are not normative but themselves require correction and supplementation. (2) Religion remains an elusive subject matter, easily reducible to data and structures, until the dimension of experience which enlivens it is clarified. This dimension of experience (religiousness) is the human response to whatever is judged to be the widest environment that disposes human life. (3) Although religion itself exists in specific historical manifestations, certain general hermeneutic principles are requisite to the study of religion. (4) "Theology" names an "understanding" that reflective encounter evokes of a specific religious faith. It can also describe the self-conscious inquiries a specific religious faith sponsors about itself and from its own perspective. (5) The study of religion and theological studies share the common problem of confusion about their subject matter. This common problem is the result of the dilution or elimination of the hermeneutic principles needed by each one, owing to certain paradigms of modern scholarship. These five considerations push us to reformulate the problem of theology and the study of religion. Given the considerations, how can religion be studied and taught in such a way that its dimensional complexity (religiousness, historical concreteness, reality) is brought to light, and what place—if any—does theology have in these religious studies?

What this reformulation has done is shift the ground from the so-called antithesis of theology and the study of religion to the hermeneutic problem common to both, which, in different fashions, attends most of the enterprises of the university at large. It is at the point of a more adequate hermeneutic of religion that the question of the subject matter of the study of religion and the relation of theological studies to religious studies can be clarified.

This chapter has tentatively identified some of the conditions necessary for such a hermeneutic. My proposal arose from a description of religion as including dimensions of truth concern, experience (religiousness), and historical concreteness. This implies that the subject matter of the study of religion is religiousness as it is embodied in concrete historical forms that constitute claims concerning the character of the widest horizon of human experience and the human problem. Apart from the presence of these dimensions, the study of religion becomes the study of a cultural curiosity, or a study of historical data and structures, or the study of some general thing existing above history and culture. Given the requisites for a hermeneutic of religion, a scholarly study of religion—appropriate to the aims of the university—will include studies of specific religious communities which engage the claim of these faiths to truth and reality and which attempt to uncover their experiential and human dimension (religiousness).

Our hermeneutic principles for the study of religion help illuminate the aims of programs of religious studies in the university. The most general aim of religious studies is the critical or scholarly presentation of religion, a presentation that involves both investigation and teaching. Because of the various dimensions of religion, however, this general aim entails specific aims. Hence, religious studies would aim at a presentation of the pluralism of historical religions, and hence, of specific religious faiths. If these specific religious faiths are considered seriously and not assumed to be mere curiosities, a presentation of them will include their claims to truth and reality as well as their experiential dimension, the religiousness they embody. The presentation of specific religions through historical and "phenomenological" comparative studies may also be an aim of religious studies. If it is, its justification would be its contribution to the illumination of religion and religiousness. When we consider the presentation of religion pedagogically, there again appears to be one general aim. It is so to present religion in its various dimensions that "understanding" is evoked. The understanding would involve historical information about specific religions and insights evoked by their claims to reality and truth and by their manifestation of religiousness.

We take up now the question toward which this essay has moved. What is the place of theology in the study of religion and the program of religious studies? We recall that theology in its primary sense refers to the reflective effort of a specific religious community to understand itself so as to correct itself and fulfill its aims, under criteria proper to that community. In this sense there are Christian, Jewish, Buddhist, Hindu, and Islamic theologies. We note that this reflective effort can occur in ways that compromise or ignore critical modes of thought and also in ways that incorporate the critical mentality.

Christian Studies

The question of the place of theology in the study of religion reminds us that present-day programs of religious studies in fact display the influence of (Christian) theology. The university scholarship of Europe from the twelfth century through the continental Enlightenment to the present day has produced a number of specific scholarly undertakings ("sciences") that have to do with the interpretation of the Christian religion. These disciplines, mostly of a historical character, have in recent times carried out their work under general and rigorous canons of historical scholarship: thus, biblical studies, church history, historical theology and the like. Although these disciplines reflect a past and present tie with the self-interest and agendas of the Christian religion, they tend not to allow that tie to replace or alter the evidences and criteria expected of scholarly work. The tie with the Christian religion is manifest in the way the disciplines appear in and structure the curriculum and pedagogy of schools, especially the schools for the training of clergy. In spite of this tie, the disciplines tend to be selectively independent of one another and, as such, frequently appear in programs of religious studies under the rubrics of the history of Western Christianity, ethics, and biblical studies. Thus, this residue of the history of studies pertaining to Christianity finds its way into the modern university. This is to say that "Christian studies," in the sense of a cluster of relatively independent fields of scholarship pertaining to the Christian religion, have some presence now in the university.

Theological Studies

It appears clear that "Christian studies" do not express an approach or perspective that is theological in character. The theological study of a religious faith is not simply a cluster of independent, historical-critical investigations whose only unity is a historical subject matter. Such a cluster, Christian studies, is in fact the historical aftermath of the loss of theology. The conventional approach to theology and re-ligious studies assumes that the introduction of a theological perspec-tive is a priori a compromise of the rigor and critical nature of historical scholarship. Such a view identifies theology with precritical modes of interpretation. What in fact happens when the theological perspective is introduced? When theology or a theological approach unifies a set of studies of a specific religious community, there is (as in Christian studies) a historical presentation of that community. This presentation occurs from a perspective of seriousness about the community's reality claims, and about its experiential, human dimension. It does not seem evident that such seriousness is a priori a compromise of the general canons of university scholarship. On the contrary, there appears to be some coincidence between the hermeneutics of a specific religious faith represented by this seriousness and the hermeneutics required by the study of religion.

The suggestion here is that both religious studies as a cluster of independent historical studies and Christian studies (or Jewish, Bud-dhist) as a cluster of independent disciplines are inadequate to their subject matter as enterprises of both scholarship and pedagogy. Both call for a hermeneutic of religion in which the specificity of religious communities is honored, their claims to reality are reviewed, and the experiential dimension is explored. Such a hermeneutic is what en-ables the study of religion to recover its subject matter.

The Problem of Advocacy

We have argued so far that an adequate general hermeneutic of the study of religion is similar to the hermeneutic of specific religions represented by theological study. To the degree that this is the case, theological study and a theological perspective may help to realize the aims of religious studies and to unify the scattered disciplines of Chris-tian studies. Does this entail a recommendation for departments of religious studies to staff themselves with Christian, Jewish, Buddhist theologians? The question itself should be avoided. Any policy about staffing a university department or science is unfortunate if it makes that question a question of constituencies. A policy that identifies adherents or nonadherents of specific religions invites the university to exclude scholar-teachers either on the grounds that they are adherents or on the grounds that they are not.

This issue is, however, still before us insofar as the conventional view, which posits an antithesis between theology and the study of religion, assumes that adherents or participants of a religious faith are disqualified from true scholarship by the *kind* of advocacy they will inevitably pursue. I assume, in putting the question this way, that advocacy is an established principle in the university: the university is hospitable to strong convictions about the importance and relevance of the subject matter and to seriousness and openness about its claim upon the student. There appears to be nothing about the hermeneutic principles of theological study which compromises such advocacy. Nor does there appear to be any reason why a participant in a specific religion will necessarily engage in a kind of advocacy inappropriate to the university. It is also crystal clear that there are adherents of religious faiths (as well as nonadherents) who teach and inquire in ways that do compromise the advocacy and objectivity proper to the university. Hence, there are instances, even in state-supported universities, where adherents of a specific religion stamp the "one true religion" onto the structure of the department of religious studies. Violations of the university's principle of advocacy are well known. In such cases the discipline or subject matter is taught from the standpoint of some single "true" world view or paradigm of knowledge and reality, a paradigm presented to the student as virtually a creed. The point is that the violation of the general canons of the university (openness, critical temper, principles of evidence) and the improper exercise of advocacy constitute a larger problem than one posed by the study of religion, and there is nothing intrinsic about either the hermeneutics of theological study or participation in a religious community that necessitates such violation.

I conclude then that there is a place in the study of religion for (*a*) the study of specific religious faiths, and (*b*) engagement with those faiths at the point of their reality claims and their experiential dimensions (of theological hermeneutics). I conclude also that there is nothing about these tasks that either requires or disqualifies scholars who happen also to be adherents of specific religious faiths.

NOTES

1. The 1950s and 1960s marked two decades of fairly frequent publication on the teaching of religion in higher education. This literature includes occasional symposia in which an essay on systematic theology was included. See, e.g., D. D. Williams, "Systematic Theology," in *Religion in the State University* (New Haven: Soc. for the Study of Religion in Higher Education, 1965). In addition there are several essays or chapters addressing explicitly the problem of theology in higher education: Alexander Miller, *Faith and Learning* (Westport, Conn.: Greenwood Press, 1960), 110; W. G. Pollard, "The Recovery of a Theological Perspective in a Scientific Age," in *Religion and the University*, ed. J. J. Pelikan et al. (Toronto: Univ. of Toronto Press, 1964); Paul Ramsey, "Theological Studies in College and Seminary," *Theology Today* 17 (1961) 466–84; Julian Hartt, *Theology and the Church in the University* (Philadelphia: Westminster Press, 1969), chap. 4; and Arthur McGill, "The Ambiguous Position of Christian Theology," in *The Study of Religion in Colleges and Universities*, ed. P. Ramsey and J. Wilson (Princeton: Princeton Univ. Press, 1970).

2. The post-World War II literature included a number of surveys and studies of the situation. One of the first was M. Cuninggim's *The College Seeks Religion* (New Haven: Yale Univ. Press, 1947), based on a 1941 dissertation at Yale. The two studies by Robert Michaelsen are well known: *The Study of Religion in American Universities* (New Haven: Soc. for the Study of Religion in Higher Education, 1965) and *The Scholarly Study of Religion* (New Haven: Soc. for the Study of Religion in Higher Education, 1965). Another study is *Teaching of Religion in State Universities*, ed. M. D. McLean and H. H. Kimber (Ann Arbor: Univ. of Michigan Press, 1960).

3. Although no full history of the teaching of religion in higher education in the United States has been written, there are several helpful works. See Cuninggim, *College Seeks*. A general history beginning with classical antiquity is Jan de Vries's *The Study of Religion: A Historical Approach* (Harcourt, Brace & World, 1967). In addition see the essay by T. W. Merriam in *Liberal Learning and Religion*, ed. Amos Wilder (New York: Harper & Bros., 1951). A very helpful bibliographically oriented historical survey of the post–World War II period is the annotated bibliography in *Study*, ed. Ramsey and Wilson. Wilson's introduction to the volume is one of the most helpful brief surveys of the period.

4. The social and cultural background of the strongly entrenched faculty of theology in the German universities is the territorial division of the country along religious lines and the tradition of the states supporting the three major

institutions that presumably contribute to the welfare and order of society: law, medicine, and religion. Hence, theology exists alongside law and medicine as one of the three higher faculties, higher in the sense of presupposing and building on the faculty of philosophy or basic arts and sciences. In the United States the tradition of religious pluralism and the disestablishment of religion prevented state support for clergy education. Hence, nothing equivalent to the theology faculty arose in American colleges and universities.

5. Specialty fields of theology, ethics, Bible (Old Testament, New Testament), American church history, historical theology, and religion and psychology attest either directly or indirectly to the Christian encyclopedic organization of disciplines. The standard encyclopedic structure is the fourfold classification of disciplines into Bible, church history, theology, and practical theology. The graduate schools retain a refinement of this structure, sometimes eliminating practical theology and adding material from other religions.

6. It is important not to identify religious studies, a program of studies, with history of religions, a certain method and perhaps discipline in the program of religious studies. Given this distinction, the problem of relating theology to religious studies is a different problem from that of relating theology to the history of religions.

7. H. Richard Niebuhr wrote an essay in this tone, "Theology in the University," published originally in 1955 and reprinted in *Radical Monotheism and Western Culture* (New York: Harper Torchbooks, 1960). The focus was on what a university would look like if it was shaped under radical monotheism, and thus on a theological portrait of the university. Similar criticisms of the university's uncritical embodiment of autonomous reason are found in McGill's "Ambiguous Position" and in Miller's *Faith and Learning*.

8. The major essays on religious studies and theology written after 1970 have tended to be presidential addresses at the American Academy of Religion's annual meeting. Two relatively recent addresses have been offered by Christian theologians, and neither of them works within the conventional formulation of the problem. Both Schubert Ogden and Paul Wiebe stress the continuity between the aims of theology and those of religious studies. Obviously, the present essay follows in that tradition. See Schubert Ogden, "Theology and Religious Studies," *Journal of the American Academy of Religion* 46 (1978), 3–17; and Paul Wiebe, "The Place of Theology within Religious Studies," in *The Academic Study of Religion*, ed. A. Carr and N. Piediscalzi (Chico, Calif.: Scholars Press, 1975).

9. The larger cultural background of the problem of teaching religion in the university is the central focus of William Pollard in "The Recovery of a Theological Perspective in a Scientific Age," in *Religion and the University*, ed. Pelikan et al. Pollard, a physicist-theologian, sees science as setting the dominant styles of thought, and he argues that this results in the loss of a whole range of reality attended to by earlier eras. What I am calling the technological or data-oriented mind-set is not so much the effect of science on modern society as it is

of a consumerism coupled with the nation-state system. In other words, the *telos* of data orientation is not so much knowledge as it is the satisfaction and maintenance of a consumer-oriented economic system that has a strong nationalistic and military component.

10. See Wilfred Cantwell Smith, *The Meaning and End of Religion* (New York: Macmillan Co., 1962), chap. 2.

11. McGill, "Ambiguous Position," 106.

12. This formulation of religion or religiousness is close to David Tracy's language of limit-experiences (*The Analogical Imagination* [New York: Crossroad, 1981], 156). Limit-experiences are primarily a negative equivalent of what I have expressed here in positive mode, that is, in the language of striving, eros, and desire. Both approaches presuppose that what we are talking about is a dimension of human existence and that it becomes specific and socially embodied with the *referent* of the eros or limit-experience as interpreted or designated. Louis Dupré cites Johannes B. Lotz's definition of the religious act: ". . . in which man knows not a particular object but the transcendental horizon of the world of objects, that is, the background of transcendent Being which is not clearly perceived in the ordinary cognitive act . . ." (*The Other Dimension: A Search for the Meaning of Religious Attitudes* [Garden City, N.Y.: Doubleday & Co., 1972], 36).

13. There is clearly a correlation between a specific historical religion's conception of the widest environment or power and the deepest problematic of human being. If Atman-Brahman is the ultimate power in Hinduism, the fate or trap of *samsara* is the deepest problematic.

14. I have attempted a historical account of the paradigm shifts of the meaning of theology, especially as it occurs in university settings, in *Theologia: The Fragmentation and Unity of Theological Education* (Philadelphia: Fortress Press, 1983), chaps. 2–5.

15. This definition is more in accord with the older meaning of theology which dominated the Middle Ages and into the seventeenth century. In that older view, theology is a *habitus*, or disposition of the mind, that has the character of wisdom or understanding. I see something like this as the primary meaning of theology. That being the case, the understanding of theology as a science, a discipline, a pedagogy, a program of studies, may be retained but as secondary to the primary one.

16. The distinction between "religious studies" and the "study of religion" is a standard one, although it is variously expressed. Ogden draws the distinction in the terms used above ("Theology and Religious Studies"). Michaelsen distinguishes between direct and indirect approaches to religion. Indirect approaches to the study of religion occur in disciplines whose primary subject matter is something else: psychology, sociology, or philosophy, for instance. Frank Reynolds distinguishes approaches to religion in which religion is studied as an aspect of some other dimension of human experience (psychology or sociology, for instance) and approaches in which religion is studied as itself a

"dimension of human life" ("Maps, Models, and Boundaries," *Criterion* 20 [1981]: 26–31).

17. A similar point is made by Dupré in his critique of what he calls the objective fallacy (*The Other Dimension*, chap. 2). He argues that the acknowledgment that religion is a *fact* does not imply that the method of studying it is simply objective method. Suggested here is that because religion is a dimension of human existence it is a strange sort of fact requiring methods able to bring that dimension into view.

18. The term "hermeneutic," which occurs frequently in this essay, is being used in a very broad sense. Its strictest and probably most proper meaning is that of a theory of interpretation that is oriented primarily to written discourse, to texts. I am using the term to refer to a theory of interpretation itself. Hermeneutic self-consciousness would be the self-consciousness about the requirements of what is to be studied, understood, known.

19. For the primacy of subject over method and a strong criticism of the fetishism of method, see Wilfred Cantwell Smith, "Methodology and the Study of Religion: Some Misgivings," in *Methodological Issues in the Study of Religion*, ed. Robert D. Baird (Chico, Calif.: New Horizons Press, 1975).

20. Given the splintering of Christian theological disciplines since the eighteenth century, we should not be surprised by the existence of scholars of Christian studies who are so narrowly specialized that they are unable to interpret Christianity itself; thus their area is a modern philosophical movement but not the Bible, Old Testament but not any major theme of Christian tradition, early Christian Gnosticism but not the larger corpus of early Christian literature, moral agency but not theology. In contrast it seems characteristic of Jewish scholars to be interpreters of Judaism whatever their specialty.

PART 2

THE STUDY
OF THEOLOGY

5

Can Church Education
Be Theological
Education?

How is it that the Christian faith, committed as it is to relating faith to
reality, world, knowledge, and learning, continues to restrict this effort
to its ordained leadership and to withhold it from the laity? Why is it
that education in the congregation and for the believer at large is so
conceived that it has little to do with the disciplines and rigors of
ordered learning? Why is it that *theological* education—ongoing studies in disciplines and skills necessary for the understanding and interpretation of Scripture, doctrines, moral principles and policies, and
areas of praxis—is taken to define something needed by Christian
clergy but never by Christian laity? In the face of the modern democratization of education and learning, how is it that the church continues
to settle for the premodern pattern of educated clergy and uneducated
laity and for the almost uncrossable gulf between theological (clergy)
education and church education? The persistence of this pattern is an
anomaly in a religious tradition that repudiates obscurantist modes of
faith and prizes learning. This chapter will explore both sides of the
anomaly: that which impels Christian faith to take ordered learning
(education) seriously, and the subterranean moves in the church's
history which produced the restriction of ordered learning to clergy
education.[1]

Faith, Wisdom, and Ordered Learning

Why is ordered learning an important undertaking in the Christian
church? If we take this to be a *historical* question, we will be asking

---

An earlier version of this essay appeared in *Theology Today* 42 (1985): 158–71.

how something born in the migrations of an ancient, nomadic, and tribal people, and at the bloody scene of a crucified Jew and the fiery tongues of Pentecost, ends up with classrooms, degrees, libraries, universities, Sunday schools, and teaching elders? History provides a rather obvious answer, but we should not be too quick to embrace it. History says that education comes from the Greek side of our civilization's ancestry. Once the Christian movement had settled into the Hellenistic world and was no longer just a house guest, it took this Greek idea into itself. There is also the sociological explanation that any movement that is to survive over time must discover the means of transmitting itself to future generations. Thus we find teachers listed by Paul as embodying one of the gifts (charismata) that ordered the life of the church.

But we need to resist explaining the presence of ordered learning in early Christianity by simply citing the Hellenistic side of our heritage. Something like education had been going on in Israel and Judaism long before the Christian movement. The Septuagint used the Greek word *paideia* to translate the Hebrew word that referred to nurture, discipline, chastening. The discipline and nurture occurring in the Jewish family was the background for the psalmist's description of God as chastening or disciplining the people. Judaism, developing a new institution of social survival and religious life in the Diaspora, made ordered learning, namely the study of the Torah, into something that occurred with special teachers (rabbis) in a special place (the synagogue). The early Christian movement did not repudiate this tradition. It modeled its own congregations on the synagogue, proposed teachers for those congregations, and in one Gospel applied the term "rabbi" to Jesus himself. The self-conscious transmission of the tradition by teachers is a deeper and older part of the Christian heritage than its roots in Hellenistic culture.

Faith and Reality

The continuity of early Christianity with its Jewish background accounts for the presence of ordered learning in Christianity only as an explanation in terms of historical influence and sociological utility. But sociological utility is here connected with self-perpetuation, and self-perpetuation can have the character of mere propaganda and ideology. We are, therefore, prompted to press our question in a different way: Is there something about the very nature of faith, as existing in the world before God, which founds in the community of faith an inclination and seriousness about ordered learning? Two issues call for exploration at this point: the relationship between faith and *reality* (truth), and the relationship between faith and *theology* (wisdom).

We are familiar with criticisms of religion as such, and of Christian faith, that argue that faith turns the human being away from reality— that faith is an opiate, a soporific. And there is plenty of documentation throughout the history of Christianity to support such an argument. Yet one of the recurring notions in the writings of Israel is the warning against deceit. "Deceit" does not name simply occasional and specific acts of trickery or of telling lies, although these things are not excluded. The word describes, rather, a posture of the heart, something virtually synonymous with sin itself. In deceit, human beings are not just telling lies but are themselves a kind of lie, a living deception. Neither does "truth" name something trivial or occasional, whose opposite is a simple error or mistake. Truth too is a posture of the heart. It is something that comes from God, who corrects deceit and redeems the heart. "Send out thy light and thy truth. Let them lead us." And in Paul truth is both something that evil suppresses and something that poses the issue of what is properly worshiped. "Wisdom," a term capturing the central theme of Proverbs, likewise refers to a matter of the heart, the very center and depth of the human being. "Teach me wisdom in my secret heart," says the psalmist. Wisdom is constituted by awe, fear, knowledge of the Lord. It is not simply cleverness or the retention of information.

Israel's understanding of deceit, truth, and wisdom attests to something very central in faith as a mode of existence before God. The fundamental brokenness and alienation of the human being is a darkened posture of the heart and mind which orients the human being toward everything in the mode of deception and self-deception. Born of this darkened posture are trickery, lying, dishonesty, intellectual dishonesty, and reality denial. Since these evils attest the absence of God and the absence of the grace of God, truth and wisdom are matters of redemption. With redemption comes a new posture of the heart, a wisdom founded in God, directed toward everything: to the other human being, nature, the self, the world in its perils and in its beauty. This is why faith's dynamics are the opposite of an opiate's. The corruption of the human being turns it away from reality and impels it to exploitative, oppressive, and destructive relations with nature and other persons—to acts that are reality-indifferent and reality-destructive. If redemption liberates from this, its effect will be an opening up to reality, a seriousness about what is and what occurs, and an interest in the autonomy, integrity, and even beauty of the world.

The second issue is the relation between faith and *theology*. Because of the unfortunate history and present connotations of the word "theology," it is tempting to discuss this issue in other terms. But the argument of this chapter is that the ordered learning occurring in congregations should be theological education. Hence, faith's relation to theology is a central issue. What history has done to the word "theology" is reduce its meaning to its objective referent (a system of doctrines and beliefs) and then narrow the location of theological activity to the specific scholarly enterprise dealing with doctrines. Given this objectification and professionalization of the term, theology has become the province of schools and of a group of scholar-teachers in schools. The narrowing of the term is now so stamped on the church and even the schools that the rescue of the word is highly unlikely. We can, however, attempt to recover the term's older meaning for the purpose of understanding why ordered learning is a concern intrinsic to faith itself. In the older sense, theology was not just for the scholar or teacher but was the wisdom proper to the life of the believer. This presupposed that faith, as a mode of existence before God, was more than an emotion or feeling—that it included a kind of knowledge. Faith was a practical knowledge having the character of wisdom because it had to do with the believer's ways of existing in the world before God.

Because faith is a response to grace and redemption and is thus grounded in the event and person of Jesus of Nazareth, the wisdom of faith has a certain natural structure. First, it has a ground or basis, something that evokes it, makes it possible. And this basis is not simply grace in general but grace as it has disposed history and a community. That is why one of the directions theological wisdom faces is toward its past heritage, its tradition—the events, imagery, history through which grace is experienced. The believer's wisdom is, then, a perpetual appropriation and interpretation of this heritage. Second, wisdom is concerned with tradition neither simply in an antiquarian way nor in the idolatrous way of absolutizing it but, rather, as the result of an orientation toward truth and reality. Hence, faith's interpretation of the vast and complex Christian heritage is always critical, assessive, appropriative. It is never merely passive or reality-indifferent interpretation. Third, the believer's wisdom always occurs in the actual contemporary setting of the believer's existence. Existing in that setting freely, responsibly, joyously, constitutes the situation of the believer. Hence, a third dimension of the wisdom of theology is the interpretation of that setting in its various dimensions. This too is why faith's wisdom is not simply directed to the past. Tradition, truth, and contemporaneity mark the ever-present aspects of theology or the believer's wisdom. Theology in this sense is a mark and task of faith insofar as faith is a mode of existence in the world before God.

Faith and Ordered Learning

What does faith's orientation to reality (truth) and to theology (wisdom) have to do with ordered learning, or education? Two extreme answers need to be avoided. The one identifies faith with knowledge (gnosis); the other expels knowledge from faith altogether. A corrupted Catholic version of the second answer sees existence before God as requiring little more than a perpetual process of penance addressed to moral consciousness and action and assisted by the church's sacraments. A corrupted Protestant version of the same answer sees existence before God as mostly a matter of a religiomoral piety taken more or less directly from the texts of Scripture as these are interpreted in preaching. To the degree that both versions expel knowledge and learning from faith, they presuppose that faith's wisdom can be formed in relation to the imagery and events of tradition, the issue of truth, and the press of the situation, apart from the faithful person's own struggles, disciplines, and insights. Thinking and insight are thus allotted to an elite leadership whose interpretations and cognitions occur above and in behalf of the believer. Any insight or understanding the believer has will be unrelated to the sort of knowledge that ordered learning addresses.

It goes without saying that anyone who participates in a living community is constantly formed by its inherited imagery and shaped by its normative events. It is a valid point that the believer's wisdom is formed in deep social processes that are the "means of grace": proclamation, sacraments, intersubjective intentions and acts, liturgy, and the structures of ecclesial organization and action.[2] But existence before God in the world is not an utterly spontaneous, prereflective matter. Human existence in the world, even in the mode of faith, is always linguistic and interpretive. Uninterpreted responses are unassessing responses, and they turn the responder over to victimizing causalities that exploit mere passivity and spontaneity. The refusal to assess a heritage absolutizes that heritage as something unhistorical and beyond corruption. The failure critically to interpret situations in the present makes the believer passively subject to the situations as if they were norms or untouchable powers. This is the primary reason that existence in the world before God requires a wisdom that is not merely spontaneous but self-consciously interpretive. It is the reason that theology (reflective wisdom) is needed. The complexity, power, and corruptibility of reality itself set this requirement.[3]

Reality does not mold itself to human wishfulness or the interiority of felt emotions. It places demands on human response and interpretation. Its complexity does not disappear in the face of human simplification. Its power to corrupt does not suspend itself before human innocence or indifference. Reality is the way things are as they are able to affect other things. The intent of the doctrines of faith is to describe realities. Great social systems and the epochs in which those systems flourish are reality. The enduring relation between a man and woman in marriage is reality. If faith is an existence in the world, it cannot avoid being a response to and interpretation of reality both as inherited tradition and as present challenge. And the response and interpretation are by believers whose wisdom is not simply others' wisdom even if it occurs in connection with the wisdom of others in the community of faith. Because this wisdom has to do with reality, it cannot avoid the rigors and disciplines that reality imposes. That is why there is a telos, an impetus in faith itself to appropriate whatever is available to it to assist its responses, its interpretations, and its insights. That is the deeper reason that the Christian faith's repudiation of obscurantism and its positive relation to ordered learning are not a mere accident of historical influence. Something about faith itself, the faith of the believer, creates an orientation to reality and, therefore, to ordered learning, that is, to disciplined efforts to equip the believer to interpret reality.[4]

Hence, faith involves a kind of wisdom, and wisdom itself as reality-related involves ordered learning. But what is "ordered learning"? Generally speaking, the term refers to the institutions or processes of a culture that communicate to the culture's members the results and methods of interpreting reality and its various dimensions in the ways characteristic of the culture. There was an ordered learning in ancient and modern Judaism, in ancient Greece, in the Middle Ages in Europe, and in the public-education movements of modern times. Since the Enlightenment, however, ordered learning has had a more specific connotation. The Enlightenment represents a massive shift in the history of ordered learning which the church ignores at its peril. This shift is not simply from premodern to modern cosmologies, or from an age of politically established religious faiths to an age of secularity and religious toleration. Enlightenment means a shift in the ways of knowing, inquiring, and relating cognitively to the world. According to the new cognitive posture, everything that presents itself for understanding and inquiry is part of a larger system or process of relations and events, and cognition and understanding are enjoined to go as far as evidence permits in grasping things in their relations, backgrounds, and historical and natural causalities. All contemporary sciences take this posture for granted. The posture combines both the principle of appropriate evidence and the principle of historical and natural relationality (relativity): according to these principles, nothing presenting itself for understanding is immune from the demand for evidence or from relationality to other things. Affected by the posture is not just scientific method in general but historical method as it would reconstruct the past, deal with ancient texts, and interpret past authorships. And all the refinements of method that have occurred since the Enlightenment presuppose the posture, including contemporary hermeneutics, social scientific analyses, and phenomenology.

The Christian church has responded and adjusted to the cognitive posture of the Enlightenment piecemeal and with continuing ambivalence. Its ambivalence is manifest in the continuing conflicts between "evangelical," conservative groups (both Catholic and Protestant) and liberal, revisionist groups. In most schools for clergy education in mainline denominations, the methods of criticism reflecting the cognitive posture of the Enlightenment are taken for granted. Hence, several generations of clergy have been educated in methods of interpreting Scripture, church confessions, doctrines, and moral issues which acknowledge the historical character and relativity of these. As a result, ordered learning has now the specific connotation of the Enlightenment cognitive posture. Ordered learning in our day is not identical with Greek *paideia* or the catechesis of earlier Christian times. The ordered learning of clergy education takes for granted the principles of evidence and relationality throughout the so-called theological disciplines.

This development adds a new dimension to faith's wisdom and to wisdom's need for ordered learning. The critical posture of the Enlightenment is available to the believer as something that assists the interpreting response to reality. That includes the believer's interpretation of the tradition or Christian heritage, the appraisal of its truth, and the relating of these to particular situations. The logic that presses faith toward wisdom and ordered learning impels that learning toward the cognitive posture of the Enlightenment. For that is what our epoch has made available to the believer in the ongoing struggle with reality.

Educated Clergy, Uneducated Laity

We are exploring the mystery of why the ideal of an educated clergy is found alongside a complacency over uneducated believers in the life of the church. The one side of the anomaly is the important role ordered learning has played throughout the church's history and the "logic" that propels faith toward reality and thus to ordered learning. The other side of the anomaly is the church's failure to take seriously the ordered learning, that is, the education, of the believer. Why is it that the vast majority of Christian believers remain largely unexposed to Christian learning—to historical-critical studies of the Bible, to the content and structure of the great doctrines, to two thousand years of classic works on the Christian life, to the basic disciplines of theology, biblical languages, and Christian ethics? Why do bankers, lawyers, farmers, physicians, homemakers, scientists, salespeople, managers of all sorts, people who carry out all kinds of complicated tasks in their work and home, remain at a literalist, elementary-school level in their religious understanding? How is it that high-school-age church members move easily and quickly into the complex world of computers, foreign languages, DNA, and calculus, and cannot even make a beginning in historical-critical interpretation of a single text of Scripture? How is it possible that one can attend or even teach in a Sunday school for decades and at the end of that time lack the interpretive skills of someone who has taken three or four weeks in an introductory course in the Bible at a university or seminary?[5]

A defensive reaction to these questions will point to the religious- and Christian-education movements, with their sophisticated literatures, the profession of specially trained Christian educators, the thousands of devoted teachers throughout the church's Sunday schools, the carefully designed denominational curricula arriving month after month and year after year as attestations of the church's seriousness about the education of the believer. Such evidence only deepens our mystery. In the light of all *that*, how can it be that the majority of Christian believers remain theologically uneducated? The gulf between theological education as ordered learning and the "education" that is practiced by the church is not a surface or trivial phenomenon but a part of the deep structures of the church's self-understanding. It involves fundamental assumptions about faith, theology, learning, and education. The question of why this gulf persists is a historical question, but its answer does not lie simply in a history of church education. Instead, we must look for certain historically originated formative presuppositions that effected and now maintain the gulf.

At the deepest level of all is the ambivalence the Christian movement has always felt about the importance of learning, knowledge, and the sciences. The pursuit of knowledge has figured in the church in some way almost from the beginning. At the same time, medieval Christendom's treatment of Galileo and Bruno, the debates over geology and evolution, and the two-century-long hesitancy to embrace post-Enlightenment historical methods all testify to the fact that the church, as someone has said, had to be brought kicking and screaming into the modern world. Continued debates over evolution and creationism remind us that the kicking and screaming have not abated but may even be escalating. The ambivalence suggests that deceit, the violation of intellectual honesty, the resistance to reality, and the fear of truth are all very much with us and always will be. They manifest the dialectic of corruption and redemption which will always characterize the church militant.[6]

At another stratum of the deep structure of the church's self-understanding is the social structure of earlier Western societies which restricts learning to the elite classes. Here, learning was considered something to be, more or less as a whole, either pursued or not pursued. In Charles Dickens's world, ordered learning marked the "gentleman" and "gentlewoman." In a social world where classes are relatively fixed, learning is for the few—royalty, aristocracy, clergy, physicians, lawyers. The association of learning with the elite reinforced the gulf between educated clergy and uneducated believers. It does not, however, account for the persistence of the gulf. The reason is that we live in a time which has embraced the democratization of learning. We now assume that public education communicates the rudiments of history, mathematics, literature, and the natural sciences to almost everyone. But even though church education is offered to a population largely educated in these rudiments, the education still fails to be ordered learning. The church continues on the assumption that ordered learning *with respect to matters of religion*, its texts, history, beliefs, and practices, is not a possibility for the believer.

Are there specific formative presuppositions that have operated beneath these two strata of the church's self-understanding to create the gulf? I have selected three themes that I think help open the mystery of the gulf: the professionalization of theology, the homiletic paradigm of the way faith occurs, and the generalizing of the meaning of education. All three of the themes have been reflected in historical movements that have left their impress upon institutions—upon the seminary or theological school, upon the preaching performed by educated clergy, and upon the religious- and Christian-education movements. Through the institutions, the social persistence of the themes has been assured.

The Professionalization of Theology

One factor in establishing and sustaining the gulf between theological education and church education has been the gradual narrowing of the concept of theology and the attendant situating of theology within the university.[7] For over a thousand years—until the eighteenth century—the word "theology" referred to a wisdom or sapiential knowledge of God. This does not mean there was utter agreement on the basis and nature of this knowledge. There were mystical conceptions of it (Pseudo-Dionysius, Bonaventure); scholastic conceptions (Thomas Aquinas), where this knowledge had the character of demonstrated conclusions; and biblicist conceptions, where the knowledge was a knowledge of God mediated through God's written word. All agreed, however, that theology was a kind of knowledge, a habitus or disposition of the believer. Viewed this way *theologia* was a part of Christian existence as such. Even the distinction between lower and higher levels of this knowledge was a distinction offered to the believer qua believer. It was not a distinction between priests and laity, between scholars and nonscholars. The story of how theology came to mean something else includes the rise of the universities in Europe and the move of theology into the university as a university science. It includes a shift in the seventeenth century in which theology came for Protestant schools to be not a disposition or wisdom but the referent and content of that disposition—in other words, doctrines, beliefs, and systems of beliefs. Once theology was located in the schools that educate clergy, it became an umbrella for the cluster of sciences and disciplines organizing that education. In a final narrowing, theology moved from being equated with the "clergy sciences" generally to becoming identified with one of them, namely, systematic or doctrinal theology. Once this narrowing took place, theology was lost even to the clergy, the ordained leaders, and came to be restricted to teacher-scholars who presided over clergy education or one of its fields. The result of this long process of narrowing is that clergy education and theology have become correlative. The school of clergy education is the primary home for theology, and the fields pursued in that school (or one of the fields) define what theology itself is: a scholarly discipline.

It is plain how this shapes the church's posture toward the education of the believer. Whatever education in the church is, it cannot be theological education, since that is what the clergy study in schools designed for their training. Church education, if it exists at all, must discover some other sort of education than education that is theological. Since the theological school as a postbaccalaureate seminary is an enterprise of ordered learning appropriating (at least in its ideal sense) the best resources of learning available, the nontheological education in the church must be conceived other than as ordered learning. Further, because education in the church must be differentiated from theological education, and therefore from theology, it becomes unable to appropriate the original meaning of theology as wisdom, discipline, and interpretation of tradition, truth, and situation. It thus becomes

believer's relation to the tradition or heritage of faith to a relation to texts and by its assumption that exposition of the authoritative text settles the question of truth. Further, its method of "application" of text to life vastly simplifies and even replaces the complex tasks of interpreting and reflecting on particular situations. In other words, the homiletic paradigm telescopes and reduces the situation of the believer and violates the nature of faith's wisdom by repressing its elements, requirements, and tasks. The reason this paradigm enlarges the gulf between theological education and church education is that it requires ordered learning for the proclaimer, the one who struggles with the texts, doctrines, and the problems of interpretation and application, and withholds ordered learning from the process of faith itself. The believer's wisdom, if it is granted at all, is viewed as a passive accept-ance of proclaimed and applied texts, and hence it does not have the character of disciplined reflection in constant struggle with tradition, truth, and the believer's situation. As passive, it is released from the deliberate inquiry and thinking expected of seminary-trained clergy.

At first sight, the homiletic paradigm appears to be a hierarchical model of faith's formation. In fact, it is not. The products of the church's learning and scholarship are not in fact communicated or "passed on" to the laity. Clergy, not laity, are the recipients of ongoing theological scholarship. What is it then that is passed on in the sermon? Insofar as a traditional acceptance of the authority of Scripture is dominant, with each discrete text viewed as a unit of a priori truth to be applied, the text must be mined for whatever can be made relevant to the hearer. What in a text lends itself to application tends to be its moral content, its lesson for life, its consolatory and therapeutic power. Hence, what is mediated to the believer is usually the tradition of piety or morality, which in more recent times has taken a therapeutic turn. And insofar as the transaction between believer and the sermon event is regarded as sufficient for faith's formation, ordered learning for the believer is thought to be dispensable.

The Generalizing of the Meaning of Education

The inadequacy of the homiletic paradigm has not gone unnoticed in the church. The history of education in the church since the nine-teenth century is a history of attempts to correct and supplement that paradigm. At the same time, the corrective movements—religious education and Christian education—have themselves widened the gulf between theological and church education. Assuming that church education should not be theological education, and offering severe criticisms of catechetical education, the literatures and institutions of twentieth-century church education so expanded the very meaning and definition of education as to create a fundamental genre equivocation.[8] Desiring to correct both the homiletic paradigm of faith's formation and the catechetical paradigm of how the tradition is taught, the religious-education movements began to treat education as the total formative social process in which faith originates and is nurtured.[9]

Few would dispute that the homiletic paradigm inadequately envisages this process. Nor would many deny that everything the church does in its inner and outer mission has "educating" (influencing, formative, nurturing) effects. But once "education" comes to mean simply that sort of thing, there are two serious consequences. First, ordered learning is no longer the primary meaning of education. Education loses its usual and ordinary sense. Ordered learning calls for self-conscious attempts, usually in a corporate setting, to transmit by means of a sequential process of disciplined didactic activity both the insights and deposits of the past and the methods and modes of thought and work that enable new insights. Education in this ordinary sense comprises teachers, students, sequential cumulative learning, and appropriate discipline.[10] Once education comes to mean a community's total formative process, virtually its sociology of knowledge, this ordinary meaning disappears and a different genre altogether is under consideration.

The second consequence is a new positive agenda for the literature, the "discipline," and the guild of Christian educators. Once education's meaning is generalized, ordered learning is identified as one of many "approaches" to or interpretations of education.[11] It becomes an approach restricted to the debates of a guild and a literature—a literary phenomenon. The absence of ordered learning in church education is hardly noticed, since "education" now means something else. The new agenda concentrates upon a "search for Christian education" in the sense of a total formative socializing, existentializing process. This search explores Christian education (total formative ecclesial process) as a possible academic discipline, its relation to "theology," the educative (formative) effects of liturgy, social action, and Sunday school, and the stages of human development in relation to formative process. It should not be necessary to say that these explorations are not only legitimate but crucial. Perhaps the great contribution of the twentieth-century church-education movement is just this focus on the elements of ecclesial process. Nevertheless, when education itself is generalized to mean formative process, the stunting assumption that ordered learning is not for the believer is perpetuated.

There are, of course, aspects of the church's institutional life that seem to relate to ordered learning. Modern churches are unambiguously committed to buildings, educational spaces, advanced degrees, teachers, directors, and curricula. Because of this, the churches offer what appears on the surface to be a genuine educational undertaking. But the essential ingredients of ordered learning are missing: subject matters with their attending methods and modes of thought; cumulative, sequential stages of learning; rigorous disciplines. Since ordered learning does not determine the agenda, the field of Christian education becomes defined by the twin tasks of program administration and developmental psychology. The curriculum becomes mired in the present and does not, like the curricula of ordered learning, start at one place in order finally to get to another place. The teacher is no longer someone with special training or knowledge in a subject matter but a volunteer willing to broker the present-oriented curriculum. The content of the teaching is not a subject matter with its own requirements but whatever is identified by the curricula or teacher as having general formative relevance.[12] Moreover, since education does not mean ordered learning, there are no measures of the success or failure of ordered learning in the church. And this renders invisible the monumental educational failure of the church at the level of its laity and congregations.

If the church ever does repudiate its inherited conviction that church education cannot be theological education, comprehensive reconstruction will be involved. A cumulative, rigorous educational process and post-Enlightenment tools of analysis and interpretation (historical, literary, social, psychological, philosophical) will have to be introduced into church education. A very different kind of church teacher will be called for. Directors of religious education will have to be more than administrators of educational programs. The educator on the church staff will have to be a theologian-teacher. But for that the church will have to reassess the axiom that it takes for granted: that church education cannot be theological education.

NOTES

1. The essential ambiguity of the word "education" is discussed in this chap. Because of the word's ambiguity, I shall use the expression "ordered learning" to designate education in what I later in the chap. call its "usual and ordinary sense."

2. A description of how the ecclesial community is the environment and mediator of reality in the forming and nurturing of faith can be found in my *Ecclesial Man: A Social Phenomenology of Faith and Reality* (Philadelphia: Fortress Press, 1975), part 2.

3. The persisting corruptibility of reality, especially as it creates structures of oppression, is the central theme of Paulo Freire's influential writings on education. It is precisely because reality is complex and corruptible that education must always be a "problematizing" that would develop a critical consciousness. Thus, Freire will not settle simply for education in its generalized sense of influence and action but explicitly calls for disciplined reflection and contemplation. Without action, education is, he holds, mere verbalism; without reflection, it is mere activism. See his *Pedagogy of the Oppressed* (New York: Herder & Herder, 1972), 75–76.

4. Education as the experience of such disciplined efforts accords with A. N. Whitehead's definition of education as the "acquisition of the art of the utilisation of knowledge" (*The Aims of Education and Other Essays* [New York: Macmillan Co., 1929], 4).

5. A number of students of the twentieth-century church-education movement speak of its failure. Thus, "Christian educators began to suspect that American Protestants as a whole were biblically illiterate and ethically uncommitted. If, indeed, some sixty million hours were devoted every Sunday to Christian education in the churches, much of the energy seemed to have been wasted" (Wayne R. Rood, *Understanding Christian Education* [Nashville: Abingdon Press, 1970], 77.)

6. Something like this dialectic of corruption and redemption seems indicated in John Gordon Chamberlin's explanation of the "denigration" and "marginality" of the education enterprise in the church. One of the powers at work in this is simply the "subordination of the intelligible content of the Christian faith" (*Faith and Freedom: New Approaches to Christian Education* [Philadelphia: Westminster Press, 1965], 16).

7. For a fuller account of the narrowing career of "theology," see my *Theologia: The Fragmentation and Unity of Theological Education* (Philadelphia: Fortress Press, 1983), chap. 2.

8. The multiple ambiguity of the term "education" is described by Chamberlin, who lists ten meanings in current usage (*Faith and Freedom*, 19). He

works his way through these meanings in order to avoid the generalizing of education, and he argues that education names an intentional process that selects what is important enough to be taught and that involves teachers and students.

9. The reason that this is a genre mistake and an equivocation is that it identifies some valid but very general *aims* of education with the educational act or process itself. Further, the aims that are frequently set forth tend to be the desiderata not simply of the educational act in its ordinary sense but of the total community of faith in all of its activities. "Development of life-styles in persons and groups" (John H. Westerhoff III, "Toward a Definition of Christian Education," in *A Colloquy on Christian Education*, ed. J. H. Westerhoff III [Philadelphia: Pilgrim Press, 1972], 68) and "shared praxis" and a "way of knowing" (Thomas H. Groome, *Christian Religious Education* [San Francisco: Harper & Row, 1980]) are surely what the community of faith hopes to happen as the total effect of its preaching, counseling, action organization, administration, intersubjective structures, and liturgy. The features of the "educating community of faith" offered by Westerhoff are clearly general features of the ecclesial community in its essence and desired telos, not features of ordered learning. See his *Values for Tomorrow's Children* (Philadelphia: Pilgrim Press, 1973), 63–64. To argue that all these things have formative (educational) effects is no doubt correct. To *define* education as that totality is to divert attention from the church's low commitment to ordered learning for nonclergy.

10. It would be difficult to improve on Whitehead's description of the specificity, rigor, and challenge of education (ordered learning): "All practical teachers know that education is a patient process of the mastery of details, minute by minute, hour by hour, day by day. There is no royal road to learning through an airy path of brilliant generalisations" (*Aims of Education*, 6).

11. A number of typologies of approaches to Christian education have been offered. In *Contemporary Approaches to Christian Education*, ed. Jack Seymour and Donald E. Miller (Nashville: Abingdon, 1982), five basic approaches are described (see esp. Seymour's intro.). These studies are very helpful maps of current literature. There is, however, some vagueness on what exactly the approaches have in common, what they are approaches to. It would not help to say that they are approaches to Christian education, since what that amounts to has been historically variable and is today not a matter of consensus. More than likely, the approaches are to the "discipline" or field of Christian education as a literary, pedagogical undertaking. Insofar as a typology regards ordered learning as an "approach," the genre confusion and the generalizing of the meaning of education tend to get lost from sight. One can then debate the issues in terms of approaches to a discipline, without confronting doubts about the legitimacy of expanding the idea of education to include a community's total formative process.

12. The aspects of institutional life that seem to suggest ordered learning all come together in the Protestant Sunday school. But the fact that the Sunday-

school movement originated in an attempt to imitate the public school and that it does have the visible features of educational space, teachers, and curricula should not mislead us into thinking that it institutionalizes ordered learning. In fact the outward aspects normally mask the absence of cumulative, sequential, rigorous learning and the Sunday school is only a pseudoschool. One can thus sympathize with Westerhoff's denial that church education should be identified with the Sunday school. But Westerhoff resists the identification because the Sunday school is a *school* (*Values for Tomorrow's Children,* chap. 6, "Down with School!" esp. 56). I would resist it because it is not. Westerhoff thinks of the turn from schooling and classroom instruction as a radical new way of thinking about education. That turn, in my view, simply perpetuates the first commandment of Protestant church education, which is the commandment not to engage in ordered learning.

6

The Structure of Theological Study: Reformulating the Problem

To explore the "study of theology" requires both reformulating the problem of how to think about theological study and offering a proposal about how to structure such study. These two tasks will occupy the rest of the book. My proposal about structuring the study of theology is more an idea about what is needed than the presentation of an ideal theological curriculum. It does, however, address tensions, anomalies, and unclear conceptions in clergy and church education which call for some rethinking and some curricular overhaul. Chapters 6, 7, and 8 suggest few specific curricular revisions but they do attempt a rethinking of theological study. The rethinking is directed toward a number of features of the current situation in theological education which call for correction, sometimes even complete excision. The problems setting my exploration fall into four areas and can be stated in interrogative form.

1. *Does the study of theology have a distinctive structure and sequence?* The exploration will draw on the analyses and concepts of the previous chapters. The structure of theological study presents us with a terrain to be mapped which is not a territory of sciences but of pedagogical areas that depend on and appropriate science and scholarship. The aims rather than the subject matter of theological study provide the initial clues for demarcating pedagogical areas. These aims are toward disciplining basic modes of interpretation constitutive of the situation of the believer. The exploratory journey I am undertaking discovers in the believer's situation certain basic interpretive modes the rigorization of which orders the structure and movement of theological study.

2. *Is there an alternative to the fourfold and theory-to-practice patterns of theological study?* The problem of the structure of theological study does not occur in a historical vacuum. Rather, current clergy education has inherited much from the past, including problematic ways of thinking about the structure of theological study. This legacy needs close critical assessment. What I present is an alternative to the arrangement of study that continues in the theological schools. It is not an utter abandonment of the fourfold pattern of biblical, church-historical, doctrinal, and practical theologies, for that pattern did embody something of the natural movement of theological study, from concern with "normative" historical reality to concern with truth and practice. But the fourfold pattern is only a formal apparatus and can be a framework for very different approaches to theological study. My approach departs from both precritical and "neo-orthodox" versions of the fourfold pattern. The precritical version takes the normative reality of theology to be apodictically true literary texts (Scripture). It systematizes the exegesis of those texts ("theology") and then focuses on the ordained leader's implementation of the resulting knowledge in the church (practical theology). In the precritical version the rationale for church history tends to lie in apologetics. It is clear that any critical mode of thinking will abandon this version of the fourfold pattern, and most theological schools in fact have done so.[1]

What prevails in most theological schools appears to be a "neo-orthodox" version of the fourfold pattern.[2] I call it neo-orthodox because of its mixture of precritical elements with historical-critical commitments. In most present-day seminaries, historical-critical methods directed to tradition, including Scripture, are taken for granted. Therefore, systematics is not viewed as a mere systematizing of the apodictic truths of tradition, and church history is not viewed as mere apologetics. Instead, these areas are pursued in critical modes guided by a neo-orthodox posture. Lost, however, is the coherence of the older precritical approach. The texts of Scripture are still thought of as something exegetically interpreted and then applied, though now by means of historical methods. The results are handed over to systematics but like a hot potato. Modern systematicians, never quite knowing what to do with the critically sifted biblical contents, go their own way, often coming to rest in some comprehensive conceptual scheme borrowed from a contemporary theologian such as Karl Rahner or Karl

Barth. Church history, free from apologetics, also does its own thing without worrying about an overall rationale and without relating its work closely to the other three areas. In a similar way, the clergy-oriented practical theological area proffers its goods in relative isolation from the other three areas. It sees its justification in the self-evident importance of training the clergy in the concrete tasks and skills everyone knows they need. In the neo-orthodox version of the fourfold pattern, each of the areas has developed a mind of its own. Dissociated from its original rationale, the fourfold pattern continues as a way of organizing more or less independent pedagogical undertakings.

This state of affairs rests, in fact, on a new rationale that combines Schleiermacher's conception of what unifies theological study with the practical temper of the new world. Schleiermacher suggested that the teleological unity of theological study, its aim, was to educate clergy, church leaders. In current clergy education this viewpoint takes the form of a theory-to-(clergy)-practice way of thinking about theological study and it provides a kind of coherence to the neo-orthodox approach by grouping three of that approach's areas as theory lying behind the practice found in the clergy-skills area. This opens the way for the model of professionalization that now prevails in the schools.

My approach takes seriously Schleiermacher's insight that a historical-critical attitude toward tradition relates the footing of the texts of Scripture more closely to the larger historical reality of Christianity. This is not to say that Scripture has no special function in the traditioning process of the church but that its function can no longer be protected from historical interpretation. Does my approach preserve Schleiermacher's clergy-oriented conception of theology? It is self-evident that all clergy education is guided by aims specific to the education of church leaders. Nevertheless, for the reasons I gave in chapter 5, I cannot accept the *reduction* of theology and theological study to clergy education. I think it important to adopt a broader view of theology, as pertaining to the situation of the believer as such. Hence, I suggest that theological study must be ordered by the interpretive activities of believers in the church, whether clergy or lay, and of students in the university.

Further, my approach displaces the neo-orthodox version of the fourfold pattern with respect to the *movement* of study. I shall argue for a movement of study that goes from certain foundational studies to studies in elemental modes of interpretation. My proposal will meet resistance to the degree that reigning guild-supported specialty fields define the pedagogical areas in such a way as to conceal basic hermeneutic modes.[3] The concealment keeps their intrinsic interrelations hidden, and that is one reason that faculty and students are so puzzled and frustrated when they attempt syntheses and applications—for instance, in senior-seminar or field-based projects. The fourfold pattern and the division of theological study into specialty fields which the pattern enables never lay bare what happens in a reflective interpretive response. Everyone knows that theory and tradition must be applied, but between theory and application lies the abyss created by the fourfold pattern and its suppression of the interpretive modes.

3. *Are there ways of describing and distinguishing fields of theological expertise which reflect the nature of theological study better than existing patterns do?* There are today confusions attending the pursuit of teaching and scholarship under the rubrics of systematics, ethics, pastoral psychology, and the like. Consider the present state of theological inquiry. With the demise of rationalistic apologetics and with the deadly struggle over the nature of philosophy itself, philosophical theology tends today to be whatever a specialist wants to make it. If systematics is not a systematizing of authoritative texts, scriptural or confessional, what is it? Confusion over what to say in answer presses many in the field to settle for scholarly description of the work of other, usually epoch-making, theologians. Scholars working in the biblical fields act as if the old federal theology of covenants were still intact when they continue to speak about the Old Testament and the New Testament. This nomenclature disguises the historical-critical shift they take for granted. Biblical theology is caught between the recognition that it is a historical undertaking—the uncovering of a "theological" stratum of an ancient literature—and the pretension that the undertaking somehow establishes the truth of the theological contents uncovered. Ethics covers a menagerie of enterprises: straightforward appropriation of social science in the study of Christianity, deontological discourse, "social ethics" (which sometimes means a method and approach and sometimes simply the focus, whatever the method, on the social aspect of ethics), and theological ethics (which now seems to be in hiding). Practical theology is more a verbal rubric and as the result of recent discussions has become fundamentally ambiguous. The

clergy disciplines seem not to be sure whether they are maintained in existence by and have their scholarly rationale in virtue of their auxiliary sciences or their connection to the other areas of theological study.

Confusions arise also when the partitions of expertise and curricular organization suppress whole areas of teaching. Today we find neglected not only topics that urgently call for thematization—for instance, the topic of basic hermeneutic modes—but also areas of study concerning the world religions and the analysis of the world situation. Shamefully neglected are important propaedeutic studies such as the philosophy of human reality. It is clear, furthermore, that the graduate schools are not the therapeutic resource for these confusions. They exacerbate the confusions by contriving ever more cognitively specialized subfields to occupy the ambiguous areas in the fourfold pattern. To say that confusions of this sort are intrinsic and perennial to cognitive and pedagogical endeavors has the ring of truth, but it is, I suspect, also a defensive rationalization of the existing scheme of specialty fields. My proposal does not so much eliminate as place in focus these confusions by criticizing the way today's division of fields deflects attention from the hermeneutic modes. Thus, the basic modes of interpretation are not taught by type, and their essential interrelation and their presence in all theological thinking and all theological disciplines remain hidden. To order pedagogical areas according to a typology of modes of interpretation would help discover the interdependence and thus the unity of all theological study. My proposal therefore directly disputes the supposed independence and autonomy of the disciplines and specialty fields of clergy education. It questions whether the specialty field is itself able to be that which structures theological study.

It would be unfair and inaccurate to say that the schools providing clergy education are indifferent to criticism or that they are unaware of the problems I have laid out. Still, their domination by guilds and specialty fields makes them victims of their structure. They can alter curricula within that structure, but they cannot rethink the structure itself. Thus they respond to action-oriented criticism by adding faculty or courses. That response is not a rethinking, nor is it an acknowledgment of the unity of all theological study. Some practical fields have a new openness to theology that is ordered by the interpretive activities of believers, but they lack a way of thinking that could help them avoid subversion by their auxiliary disciplines. Consequently, my proposal explores a way for specific areas of clergy education to embody the unified structure of theological study.

4. *Can theological study be formulated broadly enough to include the church laity and university education?* My proposal is especially directed at the most severe problem of all: the exclusion of theology and theological study from the church laity and from the university. Our historical legacy presents us with two quite different ways of thinking about the structure of theological study. One takes its cue from the educational requirements of clergy education. The other centers on the post-Enlightenment development of fields of scholarly expertise. In the former, theological study is arranged and ordered by the purpose of preparing the clergy for their tasks. In the latter, there is a partition of theology, construed as a science, into sciences. The former approach necessarily directs theological study away from church lay education and the secular university. The latter approach, in its identification of theology with scholarship, just as completely excludes theology from the reflective life of the laity and the nonadvanced student of religion. Most clergy-education programs combine these two ways of thinking about the study of theology and the scholarly and pedagogical efforts which assist that study. What I propose is a third way of thinking about theological study which neither reduces it to clergy education nor partitions it into sciences. It conceives theology to be a certain kind of reflective, interpretive activity, and its natural structure or pattern to be constituted by modes of interpretation. It follows from this conception that theological study can occur in church congregations, clergy schools, and universities. As a pedagogy, theological study disciplines modes of interpretation, and it does that by availing itself of the full resources of scholarship for the inquiry into its subject matter, the Christian faith.

In the present chapter, I offer a reformulation of the question about the structure of the study of theology. In the next chapter, I present a proposal about an approach to and a pattern of theological study. And in the final chapter, I pursue the implications of my approach and suggest ways to implement it.

Two steps of the analysis occur in the present chapter. In the first step, I describe the legacy of concepts the continuing hegemony of which has cemented a certain way of thinking about the structure of theological study. This legacy is complex and multilayered. Much of the complexity has been repressed on the journey from past to present, with the result that the very topic is now elusive. "Theology," "theological encyclopedia," "the study of theology," and "theological education" are words and phrases that worked in the past but now hide as much as they disclose. The same holds for the more formal terms: "field," "discipline," and "science." The complexity of our conceptual inheritance and the elusiveness of the topic call for some sorting-out and historical reconstruction.

It is especially important to differentiate sciences, pedagogical areas, and disciplines. These are three different kinds of endeavor. A *science* is a corporately pursued cognitive undertaking for the purpose of understanding a selected, focused subject matter; the selection and focusing of the subject matter annex or create appropriate methods. Science as a corporate, cognitive endeavor can occur in institutions whose primary aims are educational, but it can occur in other kinds of institutions as well. A *pedagogical area* is a corporately pursued subject matter that exists within some larger arrangement of subject matter that reflects the aims of teaching. High-school teachers of English occupy a pedagogical area and so do teachers of auto mechanics, real estate, and business finance in technical schools. A pedagogical area may be based on but is not itself a science. A *discipline* is a pedagogical area in which the learning and teaching are facilitated by the pursuit of scientific research or scholarly inquiry. A discipline amalgamates the aims of pedagogy and the aims of science.[4] It would, therefore, be odd to call the genetic research occurring in a large corporation a discipline, and also odd to call the English department of a magnet high school a department of science. A discipline, in short, is necessarily a pedagogical area but a pedagogical area is not necessarily a discipline. To the degree that a pedagogical area draws on and communicates but does not itself advance knowledge or the sciences, it should not be thought of as a discipline. A pedagogical area becomes a discipline only when its pedagogical aims are fulfilled in the context of ongoing research and scholarship. Accordingly, middle-school biology is a pedagogical area but not a discipline. Graduate-school, research-oriented biology is a discipline.

To understand the nature of any particular sciences and disciplines, linguistic classification is not enough: there must also be an uncovering of the historical careers that the sciences and disciplines have experienced. For today's sciences and disciplines are dense social realities that bring forward into the present the oppressions of the past. Present-day interpretations tend to minimize the density, the complexity, the oppressions that survive in present social realities, partly because any interpretation of the layered past requires simplification and a reduction to what is important and useful, and partly because centers of social and oppressive power work to hide what from the past would disclose the self-interested and oppressive character of that power. By probing into the past, we shall be able to expose, and justify a critical stance toward, many of the presuppositions that have been operative in past and present approaches to the study of theology. The first step, then, will be to examine the hegemony of concepts created by the claim that theology is a science or a cluster of sciences.

The second step, also undertaken in this chapter, will be to trace the effect of the modern paradigm of the "historicality" of everything human on the way theology and theological study are approached. This will continue the description of an inherited hegemony of concepts but will press beneath the external framework of theological sciences serving the preparation of clergy to ahistorical ways of understanding the Christian faith itself and its authenticating realities, its "authorities."

One matter must be made clear from the beginning. The question of the structure of theological study cannot be identified with questions about curricula. Curricula come and go. They are designed and re-designed, almost like hairstyles. Issues concerning curricula are of great importance, but the task they set reflects the contexts and con-stituencies of specific schools. Further, curricular patterns are the products of negotiations involving academic guilds, and academic guilds are themselves part of the inherited historical density. The present exploration, then, yields neither a map of the theological sciences nor a detailed curricular design. Instead, it offers examples of specific areas of study that would be pertinent for building a concep-tually sound curriculum. Issues pertaining to sciences (areas of schol-arly inquiry) and curricula are taken up in chapter 7, but they are not central to the proposal itself. Overall, these chapters are about the study of theology rather than theological education. I argue for a broadening of theological education from clergy to congregational and university education. That broadening is perfectly consistent with con-sidering theological education to be a genuine ordered learning (educa-tion): it is ordered learning rooted in the interpretive, active life of the believer and the interpretation of a religious faith at the point of its wisdom, its attestation of something real and true. As education, theological education brings together pedagogy, institutionality, and curriculum. The question of the "structure of theological study" is not the question of an appropriate pedagogy, institutionality, and curriculum. It is rather about what these things must attend to if education is to have a theological character. The distinction here is not recondite. The subject of any education (Asian history, biochemistry, auto mechanics) sets certain requirements for anyone who would understand the subject. A foreign language involves elements and a movement of study different from symphonic orchestration. The pattern of these requirements—a pattern that tends to persist in different pedagogies, curricula, and institutions—is what I am calling the structure of study. The pattern of requirements set by theology's very content and genre is the "structure of theological study."

Breaking with a Conceptual Hegemony: Analyses and Criticisms

The problem is how to understand and carry out theological education amid the settings, institutions, and challenges of the present. And the past is never simply left behind by the present but accumulates into the heritage of the present. All presents gather up the past. But difficulties can arise if earlier ways of understanding theology and theological study continue in the present as a conceptual hegemony, a way of thinking about theological study which dominates current practices and institutions. Little headway can be made if this continuing hegemony of concepts—one might say, model—is not identified and subjected to analysis and criticism.

The present hegemony of concepts through which theological study is understood combines two quite incompatible ways of conceiving the unity and divisions of theological study. On the one hand, the pattern of theological study is understood to be created by the aim of providing educational preparation for the ministry or priesthood. On the other hand, the pattern of theological study is understood to be created by "sciences" that come together under the comprehensive entity of theology, or theological science. Although the two understandings are clearly alternatives, both are present in the way current theological schools think about their undertakings. The conceptual hegemony springs, in other words, from a synthesis of the "clergy studies" and "theological sciences" models. I shall separate the two for purposes of precise identification, analysis, and criticism.

Clergy Education as the Unity and Aim of Theological Study

In an earlier work, *Theologia*, I attempted to trace a development that took place over several centuries: the narrowing of the concept of theology from a habitus of wisdom which could characterize the life of faith, to a school and even clergy phenomenon.[5] Attending this conceptual narrowing was a narrowing of theological study to the educational preparation of ministers and priests. The narrowing of theological study is a fact of our present historical and institutional existence, and it issues not only in a dominant idea about theological study but also in a dominant institution where that idea is maintained over time. The dominant idea is that theological study *means* clergy education, and the dominant institution is the school (seminary, divinity school) whose curricular structure is regarded as itself the structure of theological study. It is just this institutionalization of the now-narrowed concept of theological study which hardens the schools' resistance to reexamining the problem of theological study.

More specifically, how does the narrowing and institutionalizing of theological study into clergy education yield a specific approach and answer to the question about theological study's structure? The pedagogy of schools of clergy education occurs in faculties whose teaching responsibilities are partitioned into specialty fields, pedagogical areas, and disciplines. From the perspective of the institution, the justification for hiring and retaining a faculty member is his or her specific scholarly and teaching contribution to the curriculum. Criteria for tenure and promotion require competent and perhaps even original teaching and scholarship in a specific *discipline*. From the perspective of the faculty member, survival in the institution requires successfully representing a specific cognitive and pedagogical area (pastoral care, ethics, American church history, New Testament). Given these institutional expectations and career agendas, a school's curricular pattern cannot avoid serving the delicate balance of power between disciplines and pedagogical areas. Thus, to restructure the curriculum according to a set of ideal criteria threatens the existing balance of departmental power and the careers of guild-oriented faculty members. The question of the structure of theological study is, consequently, tamed in advance and reduced to the question of how the existing curricular structure might accommodate itself to student needs and to immediate concerns and dissatisfactions. It is not surprising that the pedagogical areas in the curricula of theological schools are tacitly taken to express the structure of theological study.[6]

There are strong reasons why existing pedagogical areas and the structure of theological education are not identical. First, as I argued in chapter 5, theological study concerns something broader than clergy education and its aims. The curricular organization of seminary studies embodies the aims of a special educational undertaking.

Second, the pedagogical areas of clergy education are the product of a series of historical determinations that include the fourfold theological encyclopedia of late-eighteenth-century Europe, American theory-to-application modes of thought, the relatively recent development of specialty fields cocreated by graduate programs and tenure-and-promotion reward systems, the professionalization of clergy education, and the proliferation of skill-oriented pedagogical areas. Since all these historical determinations call for critical assessment, we cannot simply assume that the pedagogical areas they have produced coincide with the structure of theological study.

Third, the pedagogical areas are socially complex in that they amalgamate pedagogical and scholarly aims in different ways. Some of the areas possess the social and professional features of a science (journals, professional societies, specialized concerns) but still do not have sufficient unity, rigor, and clarity to be either sciences or disciplines. Some of the areas are very specific specialty areas (e.g., wisdom literature of ancient Israel). In short, the pedagogical areas are too much a potpourri of social entities to qualify as a group of disciplines organizing some larger science under a well-established rationale.

We must conclude, then, that clergy education, important in itself as a specialized form of church and higher education, is too specific for its curriculum and its specialty distributions to be identified with the structure of theological study. As long as that is not recognized, the basic pattern of theological study will not come into view.

"Sciences" as the Organizing Units of Theology

Another way of thinking about theology's unity and divisions, and therefore about the way it breaks down into compartments of study, originated in the Middle Ages. On this view theology is seen not as a clergy discipline but as a science. There is some ambiguity here, because the primary meaning of "science," *scientia*, was knowledge, a habitus of the soul, but a secondary meaning began to displace the primary meaning, in which science became a body of knowledge or a field of inquiry. This ambiguity was more or less resolved in favor of the secondary meaning when the Enlightenment universities of Europe organized their faculties into fairly specialized corporate undertakings of inquiry, that is, into sciences. Theology accordingly became a faculty science like biology, ancient history, and sociology. And like them it began to develop subsciences (biblical, historical, systematic, practical). The conceptual legacy from that movement is part of the present institutions of theological studies and joins with the narrowing of theology into clergy education in shaping the reigning conception of theological studies. In the framework of this second legacy and model, the problem of formulating the structure of theological study is the problem of discovering what sciences make up the science of theology. That was the problem that produced the European movement and "discipline" of theological encyclopedia.[7]

How was this way of thinking, this notion of theology as a science or as made up of sciences, justified? Justification was found in two major conceptual frameworks. The earlier framework was the architectonic of sciences which organized the medieval universities.[8] The grounding of this architectonic was a specific way of relating revelation and reason, God and the world, the science of God and the sciences of the world. In this architectonic, theology was a single science—in fact, the apex of the sciences—but it was not partitioned into sciences.[9]

The second framework is still operative in Protestant schools of clergy education. This framework is the result of two historical strains come together: Schleiermacher's way of salvaging theology's scientific (*wissenschaftlich*) status in the university, and the new arrival on the scene, the specialty field. Schleiermacher's proposal came at the end of a long post-Reformation search for an alternative to the medieval architectonic. As we saw earlier, Schleiermacher contended that theology belongs in the university not because it is the science toward which all other sciences point and in which they all find their rationale and end but because, like law and medicine, it provides for the education of an important group of societal leaders, the ordained clergy.[10]

Theology thus becomes a (positive) science not on a comprehensive map of sciences but on a societal map of professions educated in the "higher faculties" of the university. With the rise of specialty fields—areas of scholarly and scientific expertise based on specialty-oriented graduate education—theological science becomes a professionally (postbaccalaureate) and educationally oriented cluster of specialty fields. It exists in such compartments as social ethics, New Testament studies, pastoral psychology, and patristics, and in the subspecialties of those areas.

Neither of these conceptual frameworks assists us in exploring the structure of theological study. The medieval framework, grounded as it was in a comprehensive world metaphysics, is neither available to nor viable for most modern churches and schools. Even if it were available, it would be incompatible with the modern view that theology is constituted by a number of discrete specialty fields. The clerical and professionalized framework is inadequate precisely because it is clerical and professionalized. For insofar as the specialty fields occur on a map of clergy education, they cannot coincide with the structure of theological study as such. This is the case at least if theology and theological study occur in broader settings than schools of clergy education. On the medieval view we have a comprehensive science but not sciences. On the modern view we have specialty fields whose unity and justification are found in professional education, not in a comprehensive science.

A major obstacle to thinking of the structure of theological study as a pattern of the sciences is the elusiveness and ambiguity of the concept of science. The term "science" is clearer as a sociological than as an epistemological expression. Most of us know what is under discussion when people talk about the sciences as social entities: organized corporate undertakings of research or scholarship, with a legacy of paradigms and methods from the past, and with social conditions of existence (foundations, corporations, universities), characteristic refereed journals, and so forth. But as an epistemological term, "science" continues to be at the center of disputes about reality, knowledge, and truth. Is the purest instance of scientific knowledge and method to be discovered in a priori analytic cognition, such as some philosophers believe occurs in mathematics? That view would imply that science degenerates as it moves toward the a posteriori and the empirical. Or are the natural sciences the only pure instances of science, after which cognitive degeneration begins? Is "science" a term for various territories—chemistry, physics, and the like—or a term for various kinds of cognitive inquiry? If it is a territorial term, then all sciences fall within the circle of sciences, and the totality of sciences is at the same time the totality of reality. In this sense professional studies are not sciences since their subject matter is not one of the territories. On the other hand, if science means any rigorous inquiry, it can apply to any and all undertakings, professional and otherwise, whose methods produce public cognitive results.

What then is a science? Is it a type of social reality, a focus on certain locations on a map of total reality, or any cognitive undertaking having certain features? In my judgment, to say that science is a type of social entity is a necessary but not an adequate description of science. To say that anything is a science which has certain formal features of method is deceptive, because it avoids the issue of public criteria for the subject matter of science. From that approach it follows that because logic, mathematics, definitions, and text interpretation occur in astrology, phrenology, and even alchemy, all these are just as much sciences as biochemistry and European history. Hence, although references to social institutions and to rigorous methods are necessary to an overall description of science, what gathers a science together is a subject matter, a piece of reality, the knowledge of which is publicly available and capable of withstanding continued public and critical scrutiny.

If that is granted, what will it mean to think of theology as a science? It is important to distinguish between making a case for theology *as a science* and making a case for the *wissenschaftlich* (critical, scholarly, academic) character of theology as it is encountered in graduate education. The case for theology *as a science* requires, in my judgment, more than showing that theology is able to annex the formal features of critical scholarship.[11] It also requires locating theology on a partitioned cognitive map. That is because the particular sciences name specific cognitive undertakings with distinguishable subject matters. These subject matters can be thought of as regions of reality or as territories of the world; think of the life sciences such as histology or herpetology, or the human and historical sciences such as the economics of Central America or the scholarly study of the metaphysical poets. Sciences, cognitive undertakings, occur as very specific abstracting inquiries, biting off small pieces for cognitive mastication. Humanistic, formal (mathematical), social, and natural sciences are all *specific* sciences in this way.

Are we to think of theology as a science directed toward a specific territory of the world or a specific region of reality? There are indeed areas of scholarly inquiry in theology that do appear to be sciences in this abstracting sense: the history of Israelite religion, the study of Christian origins, the history of Western religious thought. It can be argued that theology as the science of God, and therefore of the foundation of knowledge and of the world, is inclusive of all sciences. But how would the sciences gather into this totality? When we say that vertebrate and invertebrate physiology cohere in a larger science of physiology, the territory of physiology is a fairly clear although abstract demarcation. But what is the territory that theology marks off? The Schleiermacherian position abandons any notion of a world territory, since it unites the theological "sciences" by means of a set of educational aims respecting the clergy. But the clergy as such are not the subject matter, the object, the region, of inquiry. It is rather that clergy activities and responsibilities provide guidelines for pedagogical areas. In consequence, theology is not on this view a specific science on the map of sciences.

Many if not most of the people in the university will welcome this cautionary conclusion and will see it as justifying the exclusion of theology from the university's curriculum. But we must not forget that the university is increasingly receptive to studies directed toward various "professions" of society (business, law, forestry, applied engineering) and that these studies do not cohere into a single, comprehensive science setting off a territory of the world. More important, the university does and should support cognitive endeavors that are not conducted as discrete sciences but that have the character of perspectival emphases.[12]

Philosophy is a clear example. Philosophy as a pedagogical area or department will be staffed by scholar specialists (logicians, linguists, historians of particular periods), but their humanistic or social-scientific specialties will not cohere into a single science marking off a territory of the world. And it would certainly be a mistake to think of epistemology, ontology, ethics, and aesthetics as sciences within the "science" of philosophy. These branches of philosophy philosophize about human knowledge or human responsibility. But what is it to do that? Philosophy has little consensus about itself, about what it means to engage in philosophy, yet there does seem a consensus that to philosophize is not to think within one of the world-abstracting territories. Philosophical thinking—analytic, transcendental, deconstructionist, or metaphysical—is always some sort of meta- thinking, not work within the cognitive territories and sciences themselves but a higher-level interrogating of their forms of discourse, methods, and conditions. But philosophy is also more than metascience. Mystery of some sort seems to be the philosopher's business, and this wider preoccupation is what makes the ethicist philosopher or ontologist philosopher a philosopher. The university, with its preference for sciences that focus abstracted regions of reality, is always edgy about philosophy and its ilk, perspectival emphases occurring on the margin of the cognitive territories.

I have pursued this rather lengthy aside for the sake of an example of a cognitive and even rigorous endeavor which is not a world-territorial science and which is not partitionable into sciences. It appears to me that philosophy's position in the university gives us a model for understanding theology's situation. Like philosophy, theology in the academy annexes and pursues humanistic and social-scientific projects. But even when these pursuits become specialty fields (the archaeology of Palestine, structuralist exegesis), they are not parts of a science comprising subsciences. Nor is it helpful to think of ethics, theological anthropology, ecclesiology, theodicy, and the study of religious language as discrete sciences. They are, rather, ways of exercising a distinctive kind of thinking or reflection. For theology is like philosophy in having a preoccupation with mystery which resists partitioning. Theology's specific subject matters are not abstracted regions of reality but ways of penetrating the overall mystery of the world. The mystery with which theology is preoccupied does not fall into one of the compartments of knowledge or reality, since it is the mystery of these things themselves. Theology, too, is a kind of meta- thinking, and it occurs at a distance from all the world territories and their sciences. So the reason that theology cannot easily occupy a place among the sciences is not that a heteronomous revelation calls it into being. Rather, it is that the mystery with which it is concerned is not confined to one of the world's territories.

If theology is not a science, it does not subsume sciences as its parts. Theology is, however, a distinguishable pedagogical undertaking that appropriates the contents and methods of humanistic scholarship and the social sciences. Accordingly, theology in the academy may meet the conditions of a *discipline*. Theology, concerned as it is with mystery, can generate studies and therefore an organization or structure of studies.

Theological Study under the Impact of a Major Paradigm Shift

If theological study is not created and structured by the needs of clergy study or a pattern of theological sciences, then we must find a different way of understanding what theology is and how it offers itself for rigorous study. We turn now to uncovering the details of how theology can offer itself for rigorous study if theological thinking is meta- thinking. But in this, we cannot avoid confronting another legacy that works against a reformulation of the problem. Nevertheless, the critical struggle to transcend that legacy is what is required for a different understanding of the structure of theological study as comprising basic modes of interpretation. The legacy I refer to concerns what is metaphorically styled the "house of authority," and through the legacy is transmitted what is probably Christianity's dominant paradigm for understanding the grounds and operations of theology.

How does this legacy dominate present-day approaches to the structure of theological study? Theology, along with most other human endeavors of understanding in Western culture, is part of a massive, centuries-long paradigm shift from ahistorical to historical ways of understanding reality.[13] Thomas Kuhn has reminded the modern sciences that they cannot escape historicity—that is, that they cannot escape being part of and influenced by context, language, power, ambiguity, relativity, and the like.[14] A comparable message concerning academic theology has been delivered in the work of the history-of-religions school, Ernst Troeltsch, the Frankfurt school, and modern hermeneutics. The paradigm shift has roots in the European Renaissance. It is clear that its effect on theology, as well as on religious communities and the way they understand themselves, is very far reaching even though the full potential of the shift has yet to be realized. For all kinds of conceptions, paradigms, and modes of thinking persist little affected by the widespread recognition of theology's historicity by present-day theological schools. There are, in other words, both an acceptance of and a resistance to the paradigm shift, and the resistance reveals itself in the retention of pieces of the older conceptual hegemony for the understanding of theology and its study.

The resistance appears in two closely connected tendencies. The first would make religious insight and wisdom so internal to the community of faith that it results in a kind of ghettoization of theology.[15] On this view, theology is something done exclusively in, by, and for a specific religious community and its institutions. The result is that the religious community's institutions pursue their scholarship and pedagogy in isolation from the larger environment of the universities.[16] At the same time, the study of religion which goes under the title of "religious studies" is, in the larger culture, in colleges, universities, and graduate schools, relieved of the responsibility of addressing and assessing the wisdom of the specific communities of faith. It is relieved, in other words, of all theological responsibility.

The second tendency is a certain indifference to the historicity of human religion which results in a survival of precritical elements and models in theology. Behind this tendency is the precritical conviction that textual and institutional authorities have some sort of a priori truth.

These two tendencies are connected, inasmuch as the opening-up of theological study to the larger environment of university sciences would have an effect on theology's acknowledgment of its own historicity. And that in turn would help break the power of precritical ways of doing theology and assist in uncovering an approach to the structure of theological study that is not beholden to those ways.

Theological Study in Cognitive Isolation

The tactic identified by H. Richard Niebuhr as a pitting of "Christ against culture" is employed to justify an adversarial relation between the institutions of religion and other culture-bearing institutions; the goal is to offer possibly radical cultural criticism and at the same time protect the distinctiveness of the religious witness. Thus, it may be argued, seminaries for clergy education best survive and fulfill their aims when they are not institutionally dependent on larger educational institutions. There is also the correlative view that since faith and the institutions of religion (congregations, denominations, schools) provide the basis and possibility of theology, theology should have no existence outside these institutions—that it does not belong in secular universities. Grounding this view is what is sometimes called *fideism*,[17] according to which the cognitive and reality status of the witness—the images and narratives of a religious faith—is evident only to the participant, the believer, in the specific religious community. To put it negatively, the wisdom, the "truth," attested by that religious community has no evidential power, no accessibility, beyond the boundaries of the community. The implication of such a position for the study of theology is clear. Since only believers have access to the claims, realities, and truths of the religion, only they can assess them. Hence, the study of theology outside the religious community can be only phenomenal and descriptive.

In one respect fideism is on the mark. Truth, especially in the form of wisdom, originates in the historical experience of specific peoples. Moreover, as a tactic, fideism seems to offer an advantage: it protects the specificity of religious truth from false and inappropriate criteria. But is it the case that the wisdom of specific religious faiths cannot be understood, entered into, much less appropriated, in other environments than the communities in which it originated? The question has a rhetorical ring. For human beings often do experience traditions other than their own as holding a wisdom that seems right, true, and persuasive. Indeed, every enduring religious faith has already violated and transcended the principle of fideism. The reason is that specificity is not simply territorial and cultural but temporal as well. Thus, every religious community that is formed by past tradition—and all religious communities are—appropriates the wisdom of a different specific community and historical context from the present once. The wisdom of Israelite prophetism originated in a religious and social situation very different from that of subsequent times. If fideism were absolutely correct, there would be no way a religious community could appropriate its own past.

The present situation in theological schools is anomalous. Theological study is not today in utter conflict with the larger world of knowledge; it is not wholly obscurantist, existing in a cognitive ghetto. The learning of post-Enlightenment sciences—natural, social, humanistic, and professional—is very much a part of the typical school of clergy education. The way this tradition of learning is present in these schools is along disciplinary lines, which means that specific academic fields make auxiliary use of this and that science or scholarly resource. The ethos of present-day theological schools includes a general commitment to the paradigm shift to the historical character of religion. Something of this commitment is evident even in the most conservative evangelical seminaries, where the biblical faculties use historical methods. Furthermore, many theological schools are less parochial than the universities, because in embracing a more complex paradigm of knowledge and reality, they incorporate into their programs the literary, philosophical, humanistic, and praxis hermeneutics capable of correcting the narrower Enlightenment tradition of the universities. In what sense, then, do theological schools show the effects of isolation and the symptoms of fideism?

It is evident that the educational programs of the theological schools find their unity not in "theology" but in a variety of specific scholarly and pseudoscholarly disciplines. There is, then, no overall way these schools can bring the various hermeneutics to bear on theology itself. Instead, they appropriate the cognitive resources of university sciences and disciplines piecemeal, in order to serve the techniques of ministry or specific historical inquiries (denominational history, exegesis of the Book of Hebrews). This means that instead of bringing the truth and reality of the religious faith's witness under review, they disperse the witness into multiple historical studies and professional applications. The consequence is that many things going on in the social, natural, and humanistic sciences have little chance of affecting theology, when that means a normative and critical reflection on, and assessment of, the wisdom of a specific religious tradition. An overall interpretation of faith's realities would be to its own advantage shaped and critically refined by taking into account at least four areas of university inquiry that are too often neglected by the schools of clergy education.

The *natural sciences* have by and large been placed in brackets by biblicist and post-Kantian ways of going at theology. This has resulted in increasing the distance between the "realities" focused by interpretations of religious faith and the world described in physics and microbiology. Although theology and religion continue to affirm that "God acts in the world," the world theology has in mind has little to do with the world of post-Newtonian and post-DNA sciences. Thus there is an increasingly rhetorical character to theological language as it tries to relate the images and realities of the religious tradition to the "world."

Radical philosophy encompasses a cluster of post-Nietzschean movements whose common agenda is to slay the dragon of classical Western metaphysics. Within the field there are distinct historical lines of influence and development: from Nietzsche through Altizer; from Hume through Wittgenstein; from James and Dewey through Rorty; from Nietzsche through phenomenology, Heidegger, and Derrida. Each line has produced both defensive and constructive responses in theology. Each articulates in its own way the historicity (relativity, finitude, ephemerality) of human knowledge, and calculates, corresponding to that, what human beings can know and experience. Each line sees modernity—or postmodernity—as representing a radical historical shift from the Christian ontotheology and metaphysic of being to a destruction of all "realities" conceived by, or requiring what is conceived by, a "metaphysics of presence": religion, logos, truth, essences, being, God. Some even among theologians concede that theology now occurs in the time of the end of theology and argue that any genuine "study of theology" must acknowledge the arrival of that end.

Praxis hermeneutics includes all the movements since Marx—though not necessarily directly related to Marx—for whom oppressive social power and the agendas of action evoked by that power are the primary reality to be considered in genuine interpretation. The movements include Marxism, the Frankfurt school, European political theology, and feminist, black, and liberation theology. In the movements, one finds political, philosophical, and theological positions taken, and of the four areas of university inquiry that I am mentioning, praxis hermeneutics seems to have the most influence and presence in current clergy education. It, too, offers correctives for conceiving the study of theology.[18] According to these movements, no study of theology is viable that does not originate in a critical confrontation with oppressive social power.

Religious studies, a fairly recent arrival to the American academic scene, represents a self-conscious academic reform. With the rise of the public and secular university after World War II, an alternative was needed to the pervasive Christian approach to the teaching of religion which had been in place since the dominance of the church-funded

college in the nineteenth century. Religious studies is more a pedagogical area concerned with religion than any one coherent approach
to the study of religion. It places high priority on the nature of religion,
the context of contemporary culture, and the major world religious
faiths. It is hardly conceivable that the study of theology could be a part
of the present and future university without finding its place in religious studies or without discovering its relation to the study of world
faiths.[19]

The cognitive undertakings of the university have affected theological study only in a selective way, and the theological schools are paying
a price for this: their institutional independence has meant some
degree of cognitive isolation. This is not to urge that the seminaries
simply abandon their independence and merge with the universities.
Another, and possibly even higher, price would be paid for that move.
But fideism and the view that only the faithful have cognitive access to
matters of faith are not limited to the religious institutions. In a certain
sense the universities and religious studies have bought this bill of
goods. For the study of religion accedes to fideism when it teaches
religion only phenomenally and descriptively, thus denying the possibility that religious contents call for appraisal and even appropriation.
Against such a view, it should be said that the assessment of the
specificity of the wisdom of religious faiths is as legitimate as the
interpretation and assessment of any specificity: Freudian anthropology, Marxist hermeneutics, Platonic ethics. My concern at present, however, is not the university but the theological school. For the
structure of theological study to be reformulated, theology itself needs
to participate in the new paradigm shift in a more thoroughgoing way
than it has participated. As long as "theology" names a cluster of
dispersed academic and professional fields, it will continue to be
relatively isolated from the cognitive horizons of modern learning. And
that means isolation from what mediates and continues to explore the
new paradigm shift.

Theological Study in the Old
Authority Paradigm

The persistence of remnants of the older paradigm into the present
has created paralyzing confusions that have prevented theological
schools from taking up the question of theological study. One ghost that

continues to haunt the way theological study is conceived and structured is what in other places I have described as the "house of authority." The term invites misunderstanding.[20] It can be understood as a metaphor for a cluster of underpinnings that Christian theology has always taken for granted: Scripture, dogma, revelation, authority, church, tradition, and the like. Hence, to criticize it appears to be to criticize Christian faith itself or Christian theology itself. As I have used the term, however, it does not refer to these underpinnings as such but to a certain *paradigm* in which they are construed, combined, and used. It is true that the paradigm virtually defines classical Christianity, and that both the Catholic and Protestant churches have understood themselves through it. But as a paradigm, it has a historical origin and a history that include many variations. The house of authority is a precritical and unhistorical way of understanding the way the Christian community is founded in such things as grace, Scripture, revelation. To think of it as a paradigm—thus, as one among other possible ways of conceptualizing and understanding these things—is already to think outside the paradigm itself. Intrinsic to the house of authority is its denial of its paradigmatic character. The essential feature of the house of authority is its presumption that the historical vehicles through which the community of faith preserves its tradition (Scripture, dogmas, magisterium) have as such, a priori, the character of truth. Accordingly, other truths can be settled, it is thought, by reference to and exposition of the contents of these vehicles. It is conceded that further acts may be required to render the truth communicable, teachable to certain constituencies (as in preaching), demonstrable in modes of necessity, or applicable to life and action. But those activities will presuppose the truth of the contents. The contents can be exegetically expounded but may not be questioned when they are the norms and standards by which questions are settled.

Approaches that repress critical evaluation of the authority paradigm risk settling for an obscurantist or a merely formalist understanding of the structure of theological study. For the house of authority is still supporting elements of the present hegemony of concepts.[21] Identifying these elements is important to our search for an approach to the question and yield further requisites for a proposal.

According to the paradigm of the house of authority, theological knowledge is made available through specific historical bearers of divine communication: through Scripture, or the tradition of the church, or both. The primary recipient of theological knowledge is the church itself, and the believer's knowledge comes by participation in the church's mediation. Because the believer's knowledge is based on divinely sanctioned mediations, it occurs in the mode of belief-ful participation rather than the mode of privileged knowledge *(scientia)* that belongs to the doctorate and episcopacy of the church. In the Protestant churches there is the distinction between ministers of the Word, who are qualified to interpret exegetically the contents of revelation, and those whose knowledge occurs by virtue of the ministers' interpretive mediation. The study of theology, then, comes to be study oriented toward acquiring the privileged knowledge of the ordained leadership, knowledge requiring exegesis and demonstration. Theology, then, comes to be this privileged knowledge, and its study comes to be located in schools for priests and ministers.

The Enlightenment had a major effect on the conception of theological study as a single science. In the major branches of Protestantism, the effect was not, however, a direct challenge to the house of authority. Instead, the various resources, tools, and even sciences that had been developing since the Renaissance were introduced into the study of theology, so that the one science became a cluster of clergy sciences: biblical, systematic, church-historical, and practical. Although the fourfold scheme was not an utterly coherent expression of the house of authority, the scheme for the most part prospered within it. Hence, the view was that the biblical sciences expound the authoritative texts. Symbolics and church history prepare the way for systematic theology by comparing the church's confession with other confessions and by placing the church, in its denomination or branch, against its historical background. Systematic, apologetic, and moral sciences—sometimes working under a second authority, the church confession—formulate the contents of the authority in the form of doctrines and defend their cogency against heretical and heterodoxical opinions. Practical theology explores how the ordained leadership can function to maintain and spread the saving truths of the church and gospel. Each of these theological sciences is built on the assumption that interpretation is a single activity directed toward the authoritative texts. Hence, in spite of the Enlightenment's dispersal of theology into four basic sciences, the paradigm of the house of authority persisted.

The approaches to theology that take it to be a single science, as classical Catholicism did, or four sciences, as post-Enlightenment Protestantism did, no longer rule in their original forms. Because of the continued dominance of the fourfold scheme of "sciences," it may look as if clergy education today follows the longstanding Protestant approach. But in fact it departs significantly from that approach while retaining its schematic and some of its conceptions.[22] The reason is that the historical character of religion, faith, and the church is now taken for granted by most current clergy education.[23] The shadow of the house of authority is cast upon the schools, but only a shadow.[24] The primary sign that the schools are breaking free from the paradigm of the house of authority is that none of the four basic pedagogical areas today sees itself as simply interpreting exegetically, defending, or applying the revealed truths. What is more, all of them have attached themselves to auxiliary sciences that have established their independence as guild-supported enclaves of teaching and scholarship: language studies, philosophical movements, the history of particular periods, psychology, management theory. These enclaves do their work not through the concept or framework of the authority paradigm but as relatively independent entities in a curriculum whose end and justification are the preparation of clergy for specific responsibilities. The pedagogical areas of the clergy schools combine, then, remnants from the house of authority with the new technologies of ministry.

It is not a stable, clear, or theologically justified pattern. The areas are stretched between the auxiliary sciences and the conviction they should be serving their tradition; furthermore, the orientation of their work toward future clergy responsibilities hides from them the abyss, the hole, at the center of clergy education. There is simply a silence on the question of what one should do with the contents of the tradition (the truths, doctrines, mythoi, primary symbols, metaphors, claims) in the operation of any individual pedagogical area: in systematic theology, pastoral psychology, social ethics, church polity. Available to the schools is a rhetoric that urges a communication of the ancient truths to the modern world. What is hidden by the rhetoric is that there is not available a postauthority paradigm for doing this which is clear and cogent. This hole may be as responsible as anything else for the ease with which clergy schools have adopted a vision of themselves as programs of professional, technological instruction.

Because of its precritical and antihistorical character, the paradigm of the house of authority is incompatible with any mode of thought that takes for granted the historicity of all human doings. Therefore we must make every effort to formulate the problem of the structure of theological study outside that paradigm. But what happens when we approach the study of theology without making use of the authority paradigm? A virtual sea change occurs, and everything is, if not eliminated, altered: revelation, authority, doctrine, Scripture, Christianity, magisterium, tradition, education. In the sense of being subject to situational, changing, and fallible historical processes, all the classical texts are seen to be "historical." Historical too are the events and persons that produced them and the institutions that continue to maintain them by ongoing reinterpretations and policies of enforcement. Historical is the *act* in which individual believers and churches understand themselves. Historical is the message to which they attest and by which they are shaped. All this tells against the idea that a faith's truths can be warranted a priori by virtue of their location in historical carriers, for instance, certain texts.

Historical, thus, is theology itself. It may continue to be knowledge, but if it is the wisdom, the understanding, and insightfulness that occur when the human being is shaped in a redemptive way, it occurs in connection with the believer's or church's responses to things, and as such it has the character of interpretation. That is, critical responses involve complex acts of interpretation. And what is interpreted is not simply one thing, the authoritative text, but everything that presents itself: the tradition, the local or even global situation, the paradigms that are disposing the interpretation, the acts and communications of other people.

There is a shift when theology and the study of theology occur outside the authority paradigm. It is the shift from theology as a cluster of sciences based on a priori authority to theology as historically situated reflection and interpretation. The outcome of that shift is that the structure of theological study or pedagogy is recognized to be determined by basic modes of interpretation rather than by sciences. Instead of being a structure of sciences or of pedagogical areas created by the aims of clergy education, the structure of theology becomes a structure of basic modes of interpretation. This is the thesis to be explored in the next chapter. The moves of the present chapter add up to a reformulating of the problem of theological study. If theology itself is not a clergy-education pedagogy nor one of many "sciences," discerning that structure cannot therefore be a matter primarily of arranging clergy-education curricula or organizing theological sciences. If theology is to reflect a postauthority paradigm of historicity, theological study cannot be the study of how a textual or ecclesiastical authority, true a priori, is rendered coherent and applicable. Accordingly, the reformulated problem is how to discern a way of understanding theological study as something properly occurring in but also beyond theological schools, and as something fully participating in the historicity of theology itself.

NOTES

1. The term "critical" in its narrowest sense refers to a commitment to invoke considerations of evidence, as against mere authority, in determining what is and is not real. This is the critical principle of the Enlightenment expressed in a formal way. In a broader sense, "critical" refers to the whole Enlightenment tradition with its various hermeneutic corrections. To be precritical in the narrow sense is not to have reached the stage of letting evidence prevail over authority—thus, for instance, to allow Genesis 1 to settle the question whether species evolve. To be precritical in the broader sense is to suspend or ignore some or all of the heritage of the Enlightenment tradition—for example, praxis, romantic, and other hermeneutics. For elaboration, see chap. 1 above.

2. Historically speaking, "neo-orthodox" is a loose and perhaps unusable term. It tends to be temporary nomenclature for what for a short time seems a movement and an agenda but quickly disperses. The term remains loose in my usage and refers to a rather broad type or genre of theology, one that mixes the language and intent of classical Christian theology with commitment (in some sense) to critical and historical considerations. Neo-orthodox theologians, Catholic or Protestant, and neo-orthodox schools resist identification equally with "liberal theology" and with fundamentalism.

3. For the concept of specialty fields, and further elaboration of other terms used in this chapter, see chap. 3 above.

4. This way of distinguishing disciplines and sciences has an etymological warrant. The term "discipline" has connotations of training or instruction, because of its Latin roots. *Discere* means "to learn," and *discipulus* is a pupil or learner. *Disciplina* refers to instruction; hence, a disciple is a scholar, a follower of a teacher. "Science," on the other hand, comes from a Latin term that translates the Greek word for knowledge, *episteme*. *Scientia* can refer to the act or state of knowing or to a specific undertaking of knowing, *a* science.

5. See my *Theologia: The Fragmentation and Unity of Theological Education* (Philadelphia: Fortress Press, 1983), chap. 2.

6. The legacy of scholarly or scientific disciplines is both the opportunity and the burden of current theological study. It is the opportunity because it has opened up new worlds of knowledge and methods about the Christian past, about history, human being, and nature, the loss of which would return theology to a cognitive Stone Age. It is a burden insofar as the guild disciplines so powerfully govern the distribution of scholarly labor that they suppress the theological question of the structure of theological study. In a work written almost twenty years ago, Karl Rahner complained that the great enemy of the reform of theological studies was *Fachegoismus,* the egoism attending the scholar's allegiance to the field *(Zur Reform des Theologiestudiums* [Freiburg: Herder & Herder, 1969], 35).

7. The interpretation of theology as a science continues to be more a German than a North American tendency. See, e.g., Anton Grabner-Haider, *Theorie der Theologie als Wissenschaft* (Munich: Kösel-Verlag, 1974); G. Sauter, *Theologie als Wissenschaft* (Munich: Chr. Kaiser-Verlag, 1971); H. Siemers and Hans-R. Reuter, *Theologie als Wissenschaft in der Gesellschaft* (Göttingen: Vandenhoeck & Ruprecht, 1970), esp. Siemers's essay; M. Gatzemeier, *Theologie als Wissenschaft,* vol. 1 (Stuttgart: Friedrich Frommann Verlag, 1974–75), chap. 5; and B. Casper, K. Hemmerle, and P. Hunermann, *Theologie als Wissenschaft: Methodische Zugänge* (Freiburg: Herder & Herder, 1970). The claim to *Wissenschaftlichkeit* here is based on the argument that science as a human transaction with reality is hermeneutic and that theology is likewise a mode of understanding able to be explicated in scientific fashion. See Wolfhart Pannenberg, *Theology and the Philosophy of Science* (London: Darton, Longman & Todd, 1976), part 2. Untypical is Dietrich Ritschl's treatment of the subject, where *Wissenschaftlichkeit* is only one of three modes or types of theology *(Zur Logik der Theologie: Kurze Darstellung der Zusammenhänge theologische Grundgedanken* [Munich, 1984]).

8. See G. R. Evans, *Old Arts and New Theology: The Beginning of Theology as an Academic Discipline* (Oxford: Clarendon Press, 1980). Needless to say, there were different versions of this architectonic in the Middle Ages, most of them dependent in some way on Aristotle's classification of sciences into theoretical, practical, and productive. The major classifications are offered by Isadore of Seville, Hugo of Saint Victor, Thomas Aquinas, Bonaventure, and Vincent of Beauvais. All the schemes place the sciences of *theoria* at the apex, with theology their destiny and end, and technical, applied, mechanical sciences at the bottom.

9. In the Middle Ages *pedagogical* stages were acknowledged in the study of theology itself; thus the movement was from the *lectio* (text studies) to the *questio* (dialectical studies). But these studies were not seen to be discrete *sciences* within theological science. The same holds for distinctions based on

adjectival modifications of theology into speculative, mystical, moral, and other types. These represent focusings of the one science, not subsciences.

10. For an exposition of Schleiermacher on the study of theology, see *Theologia*, chap. 4.

11. This way of making the case for theology as a science is not infrequent. For instance, Anton Grabner-Haider identifies being *a* science with fulfilling certain formal criteria such as explication and hypothesis *(Theorie der Theologie*, chap. 1). Hence, if he can show that theology has these formal marks, he has, in his view, made the case that theology's genre is that of a science. This formal approach prevents him from discussing theology as a particular science on a map of sciences, a particular science with a discrete object or subject matter and divisible into sciences. He in fact divides theology into four "disciplines," which he seems to identify with sciences, but he offers no description of the general science of which they are a part except in terms of the formal features directed to religious faith-language.

12. For discussion of the category of perspectival emphasis, see pp. 32ff.

13. The theme of "theology in a new paradigm" has become the primary exploratory topic of the Workgroup in Constructive Theology, an annual gathering of some twenty-five theologians. Stimulating the adoption of this theme was an article, initially a working paper for the group, by Langdon Gilkey ("The New Watershed in Theology," in *Society and the Sacred* [New York: Crossroad, 1981]).

14. Thomas Kuhn, *The Structure of Scientific Revolutions* (Chicago: Univ. of Chicago Press, 1961).

15. See James Gustafsson, "The Sectarian Temptation: Reflections on Theology, the Church, and the University," in *Proceedings of the Catholic Theology Society* 40 (1985): 83–94.

16. In North America it is usual for the seminary not to be part of a university, but there are significant exceptions. Several universities in Canada have theological schools attached to them. In the United States, there are four nondenominational university divinity schools, and a few Methodist and Catholic universities have divinity schools or seminaries. Further, some independent seminaries (e.g., Union Theological Seminary in New York) have close relations with adjacent universities.

17. On the term "fideism" and for a selected bibliography, see my *Ecclesial Man* (Philadelphia: Fortress Press, 1975), chap. 3 n. 2.

18. The concern of two recent feminist publications on theological education is with the redemption of theological pedagogy by foundation conversations that must first address the patriarchal ethos of the theological schools before tackling the issue of the structure of theological study. See Cornwall Collective, *Your Daughters Shall Prophesy: Feminist Alternatives in Theological Education* (New York: Pilgrim Press, 1980), and Mudflower Collective, *God's Fierce Whimsy: Christian Feminism and Theological Education* (New York: Pilgrim Press, 1985). On black theological education, see James H. Evans, Jr., " 'I Rose

and Found My Voice': Black Church Studies and Theological Education," in *Theological Education* 21 (1985), 49–72; and Charles Shelby Rooks, "The Vision, Reality, and Challenge: Black Americans and North American Theological Education, 1959–83," in *Theological Education* 20 (1983): 37–52.

19. On the issue of the relation of theology to the study of religion, see chap. 4 above; for a selected bibliography, see chap. 4 nn.

20. For an extended treatment of the theme of the house of authority, see my *Ecclesial Reflection: An Anatomy of Theological Method* (Philadelphia: Fortress Press, 1982), part 1.

21. For an elaboration of the way in which current clergy education and the fourfold pattern retain precritical elements, see my *Theologia*, 137–38.

22. The schematics of the fourfold pattern originate in the late eighteenth-century European attempt to transform pedagogical areas based on a pre-critical version of authority into *wissenschaftlich* or scholarly areas—in other words, into sciences. Once the sciences took over, governed as they were by the Enlightenment temper, the scheme remained but each area or science went its own way.

23. Most North American Catholic seminaries will differentiate their approaches to clergy education from the old precritical, manual theologies and from the Roman Thomist approach. Most Protestant faculties, even those in relatively conservative denominations, will be quick to distinguish their approaches from fundamentalism, uncritical popular religion, and wooden confessional orthodoxy.

24. Concepts that carry pre-critical baggage abound. "Exegesis," washed clean of fundamentalist overtones by historical-critical methods, still reflects a way of thinking about Scripture that partitions it into units of application, as if somehow authority resided by necessity in each unit. The language of Old and New Testaments connotes a precritical federal theology and devaluates in an essential way the texts of Israelite religion and their function in Christianity. It also implies that biblical fields are unified by texts rather than the larger historical phenomenon that is the actual subject matter of these areas. "Hermeneutics," in its narrowed meaning of a science of text interpretation, defines the theological task as a search for new and sophisticated ways of retrieving authoritative texts. The teaching of preaching still seems to be dominated by a text-to-sermon way of thinking about preaching, and thus a whole pedagogical area is built on the suppression of the truth question about biblical contents.

7

The Structure of
Theological Study: Mapping
the Terrain

Chapter 6 ended with a thesis. Theological study must be organized by the fundamental modes of interpretation. This conclusion appears unavoidable if we acknowledge that theology is primarily the wisdom and critical reflection attending faith. To put it statically, theology is a wisdom that constitutes the cognitive dimension of faith. To put it dynamically, it is wisdom as a reflective activity that should attend the believer's existence and action in the world. Human responses to things occur in degrees of self-conscious reflection. They range from very low degrees of awareness and virtually knee-jerk, reflexive responses, to highly deliberate, self-conscious, even investigative acts. Deliberate reflection is critical, assessive, and reality-oriented. In the operations of deliberate reflection, intuitions are refined, claims are pressed, and language is interrogated. These activities can occur in connection with the responses of everyday life, and as such are not synonymous with scientific research or scholarly inquiry. Accordingly, hermeneutics— the study of interpretation—can no longer be restricted to the interpretation of texts.[1]

But what exactly do reflective responses have to do with interpretation? Reflective activity is unavoidably interpretive activity. All self-conscious responses are at some level interpretations: interpretation is simply the way human beings respond to things. Interpretation should not be reduced to a methodologically ordered, step-by-step act. It can be that, but in the ordinary situations of life it is simply our way of construing things, our "reading" of the situations in which we find ourselves. Interpretation itself is a complex act even if it appears to be instantaneous and simple. It includes focusing on what we are construing (the delivery truck approaching our house, the line of a poem), apprehending through the language (which as Derrida says is "always already there"), appraising significance—the grade of importance—of the focused matter at hand, placing the matter against its background and in relation to other things, planning future action.

These are, of course, only a few of the many facets of interpretation. When reflective activity becomes deliberate, self-conscious, and critical, it refines and extends these doings and takes on others. Because reflective interpretation is ordered toward many kinds of responses constitutive of human life and existence in the world, it never has only one kind of aim, for instance, description. Rather, it may have aims as varied as appraisal, the estimation of an outcome, and discernment of responsibility. As a self-transcending, reflective activity, interpretation will interrogate the grid of language, question the initial belief-ful granting of reality or bestowal of attributes, place a content in time so as to consider its past and future. In other words, reflective interpretation has a critical character. It is an ongoing human activity directed to anything and everything that can come under consideration. It cannot be restricted to the past or to texts of past and present.

What does reflective interpretation have to do with *education?* Reflective interpretation, since critical, is normative, reality-oriented, interrogative, curious, and assessive. It therefore calls for assistance and can be "disciplined," made rigorous. What can be made rigorous are reflective interpretation's *ways* of fulfilling its various critical aims. Some of the aims require fairly precise knowledge, knowledge other than the practical knowledge of everyday life. Some aims require knowledge of the past and the ability to interpret the past. For instance, the interpretation of the oppressive power encountered in the world today is assisted by what Nietzsche called the "genealogy" of existing conditions. Some aims require a formal, analytical sorting-out of language uses, some the "reading" of metaphors and the structure of narratives. All this is to say that reflective interpretation has itself a historicity. It occurs at different levels of critical rigor and of success and failure. Because its aims can be assisted, it can be aided by teaching and ordered learning. Ordered learning does not create human reflective life. It instead disciplines and rigorizes reflective activity. The relation is the same between theological reflective interpretation and ordered learning. Ordered learning does not create either faith or the reflective responses to faith, that is, theology. It can, however, give faith's reflective interpretation tools and knowledge that will assist it in its constant negotiations with the complexities of reality. That is why theology, the reflective interpretation of faith, should occur in a pedagogical mode. Pedagogy or study both disciplines and rigorizes reflective interpretation.

Modes of Interpretation as the Ordering Realities of the Study of Theology

Dimensions and Interpretations

The aim of education is sometimes thought to be the transmission of knowledge concerning a content or subject matter. But when we ask about the purpose of the transmitted knowledge, we are referred to another order of aims, an order having to do with the use, function, and relevance of knowledge. Knowledge, in other words, lends itself to various agendas that attend human life, and it can improve the ways human beings exist in the situations of life. Human life is constituted by a succession of *situations* that call for understanding and interpretation. "Understanding" is the more static, "interpretation" the more active, expression. The educational process, when successful, refines and disciplines the ways of understanding and interpretation.[2] Ordered learning never begins with nothing, a blank sheet. Interpretation and understanding are not created by education ex nihilo. Rather, ordered learning appeals to and builds on already-formed understandings and interpretive responses, and rigorizes specific types of interpretation and understanding: think of the study of mathematics, literature, science, philosophy, and the like. Here there are not just bodies of knowledge but also basic types of understanding and interpretation. A grading of some types of understanding and interpretation as elemental and more important than others figures in any actual educational system of a culture. It determines that culture's *paideia*.

A great multiplicity of interpretive acts attend and guide the activities of everyday life. They reflect and correspond to different sorts of situations: working in a factory, shopping, worshiping, attending a concert, living in a family. These situations are less amalgams of contents presented to our cognition than they are composite *dimensions* to be understood and interpreted. Dimensions here are aspects of a situation which differ from one another in genre or type. A specific human response or act in a situation will synthesize these aspects. For example, the relatively simple act of conducting a bank transaction brings together realities of very different orders: human interactions, sense perceptions, and location in a certain space, appraisals of importance, expectations, motivations, aims, social proprieties of the banking world, and more. Besides, these different aspects, or dimensions, call forth different kinds of *interpretations*, which tend to mesh in the activity of the transaction. What allows there to be education—what enables the disciplining of interpretation and the refinement of understanding—is that it is possible to abstract the different kinds of interpretation. That is, the various dimensions of human life can by conceptual art be so separated that they can be focused on, analyzed, and subjected to inquiry. It is possible to lift out and subject to further disciplining the order—and with it our understanding—of, say, our personal finances, or our personal aims and motivations as they guide response and interpretation, or the world of social propriety which is part of the world of banking. Dimensions, then, are the abstractable aspects or orders of situations. *Modes* of interpretation name abstractable kinds of interpretive acts which these situations evoke. What the educational process attempts to discipline, assist, refine, empower, and make more self-conscious and efficient are the human modes of interpretation.

Elemental Modes of Interpretation

The realities of the everyday world, whatever they are, are experienced in a succession of situations. The complexity of reality, its irreducibility to any one genre or order of things, can be spoken of as dimensionality of these situations. And these dimensions set requirements on anyone who would understand and interpret them. They do not permit any and all interpretations but evoke interpretations appropriate to their genres. Hence, basic *types* of interpretations arise which can be identified and described. Thus, one set of requirements pertains to the interpretation (understanding) of what is past. Another set of requirements pertains to the ecology of the planet. There are, in other words, elemental types of interpretation which tend to appear and reappear in human history; they reflect perennial or recurring situational dimensions that are typically human and historical. It is characteristic of human beings to retain and interpret their past, especially their corporate and narrative past. And the human striving to survive, to secure oneself, to obtain a certain well-being, prompts interpretations oriented to the truth of things—for instance, to the behavior of the hunted animal, to the regularities (and irregularities) of nature, to the resources for healing.

There are, it seems, elemental interpretations in a very formal and general sense which reflect very elemental types of situations which are characteristically human. In addition we can speak of interpretations which are basic to particular types of situations. This is because very specific situations have their "elemental" dimensions and these dimensions evoke the interpretations appropriate to them.

The Dimensions of Faith

It would be misleading to call faith or faithful existence a situation of human life. But if faith is a comprehensive mode of existence, it is a way of having, living in, and responding to situations. Under consideration here is a particular form of faith; Christian faith, at least in its ideal expression, means existence—social and individual—in the mode of redemption. If redemption is construed as simply flight from the world, a repudiation of the worldly, it will have little to do with life situations. In fact, however, the very structure of redemptive existence involves a relation between world realities (creation), and it involves the fragility of these realities, human corruption (evil), and the pursuit of freedom from both fragility and corruption. Redemption, accordingly, is essentially a way of being in the world—in history and society.

Faith is not a discrete life situation but a way of being in life situations.[3] If this is the case, then the elemental dimensions of life situations are not replaced by faith. Thus, such dimensions of situations as bank transactions, living in a family, voting in elections are not displaced by a "faith situation." Instead, faith brings new features to every situation. New dimensions are introduced into life situations because of faith—new dimensions opened by redemption itself and how it occurs. Redemption is to the Christian unthinkable without the historical event, community, and tradition in which redemption is communicated and mediated (ecclesia); without the imagery and vision of the goodness, fragility, corruption, and hope of the human condition

under the transcendent (gospel); and without a praxis-oriented existence, an existence in and toward the world in modes of obligation,
forgiveness, and liberation (faith). Ecclesia, gospel, and faith become
dimensions of the situations in which the Christian believer exists.

"Dimension" is a better term for these things than "quality," "attrib-
ute," or "part." It indicates something constitutive and essential that
involves a distinctive order or genre but that is not an independent
entity, enmeshed as it is with other dimensions. Each of these dimensions is present because of redemption. Ecclesia represents the way
redemption occurs, namely, through participation in a community of
faith whose institutional and textual memory mediates a historical
drama. Gospel embodies not just the historical content of this past,
with its institutions, its texts, its story, but the reality attested to by
these things, a truth about things.[4] Gospel, accordingly, is not synonymous with its historical mediators. Faith comprises redemption as a
mode of existence, with all that this entails—and thus the way tradition
and gospel have to do with norms, warrants, idealities, and aims for
action. Without ecclesia nothing would have occurred to make redemption possible or give it any content whatever. And without a content as
a bearer of truth, the only reality reference that redemption involved
would be to the life situations in which it occurred. Without gospel,
tradition and faith would occur simply in the mode of indifference,
since they would have nothing to do with the actual life and practice of
human individuals and communities.[5]

Faith's Elemental Modes of Interpretation

My question is, What are the basic or elemental interpretations that
occur in connection with faith? The ways that the dimensions of faith
exist in human situations point to and require basic types of interpretation. The *paideia* or education of the believer is a disciplining of the
interpretation of the events and texts of tradition, of the interpretation
of the vision or content under the posture of truth and reality, and of
the interpretation of these things under the posture of praxis or action.
These, then, are elemental types of interpretation that attend the
situation of the believer and, therefore, that persist in the community
of believers, the church. Happily, the interpretation of tradition, the
interpretation of the gospel, and the interpretation of praxis can them-

selves be abstracted and subjected to rigorous disciplining—can themselves be the objects of reflective interpretation.[6]

It should be evident that all three of these elemental types of interpretation are primordially present in faith and are not just created by education or scholarship. Typically, they are present not in separation from one another but as interrelated aspects of the believer's interpretive responses.[7] They inhere in, and determine, one another. But as *types* of interpretation in correlation with distinguishable dimensions of faith, they set their own requirements on the interpreter. And these requirements can be looked at in themselves and subjected to disciplining. That is what happens when principles or rules for interpreting texts (e.g., Scripture) are proposed. The requirements for that type of interpretation are not identical with those for interpreting other kinds of situations—for instance, moral situations of proposed political violence or of proposed euthanasia.

Because these types of interpretation attend the dimensions of a faith that has endured for many centuries, they have long been the subject of the church's education. Disciplining, inquiry, and scholarship have been brought to bear on the elemental types of interpretation in the church. The house of authority has been the dominant paradigm for understanding the kinds of interpretation that matter for faith. In that paradigm, the interpretation of the content of tradition, especially of the content carried in authoritative texts, has been identified with the establishing of that content as true. Hence, "dogmatics" means the rendering of the true content into a comprehensive coherence and also the apologetic defense of the content. The paradigm of the house of authority founds one version of the theory-to-practice approach to the structure of theological study. In other words, the essential threefold structure of interpretation in faith's situation is reduced to the duality of authoritative text and application.

It would be premature to conclude that this threefold structure constitutes the structure of theological study. Because the three elemental types of interpretation so far identified reflect interrelated dimensions of faith, they are interrelationally copresent. But what do they coinhere in? Clearly, they coinhere in that which all basic types of interpretation occur, namely, in a comprehensive response to, or way of existing in, situations. Accordingly, the interpretation and the disciplining of interpretation that are connected with faith are not limited to these three elemental types. There is also the comprehensive interpretive act of the believer, the interpretation of situations. The neglect of this marks what is probably the great lacuna of church and clergy education. Given the modern fascination with applications, with relevance and the practical, it may be its great irony. For, whatever the historical reasons, interpreting situations as a comprehensive act has not managed to rise to hermeneutic consciousness. Because of the hegemony of the sciences and pedagogical areas, the interpretation of situations is present in clergy education only under the auspices of the disciplines: thus psychological studies of death in pastoral care, sociological studies of the church in social ethics, and eschatological studies of the global crisis in theology. We must not dismiss the importance of the perspectival, focused, and categorical contributions that the disciplines bring to the interpretation of situations. But the disciplines never thematize what it means to interpret situations in the light of the basic dimensions, and the elemental types of interpretations, of faith.

Thus a basic, elemental type of interpretation, a fourth type, seems to be missing from church and theological education. This is the kind of interpretation that occurs constantly in the concrete life of the believer and in the corporate life of the church. It is the interpretation in which the other elemental types of interpretation distinctive to faith come together in concrete acts. If this type of interpretation became the subject matter for inquiry and pedagogy, there would have to be a concern with the formal or general structure of any situation and with hermeneutics as such, that is, with the distinctive way all the basic types of interpretation come together and function in the interpretation of situations involving faith. When this set of issues is ignored, interpreting situations can be dominated by casuistry, or by naive biblicism, or by culture-legitimating approaches. One of the spinoffs of feminist, black, and Third World theologies is the imperative to investigate the hidden side not just of the interpretation of tradition and action but also of the comprehensive interpretation of situations.

The failure to render thematic the interpretation of situations as such has resulted in another serious lacuna: a failure to understand fully the nature of vocations and the role of vocations in the life of faith. It goes without saying that life situations do not occur successively in a flat series in which each situation has equal weight. Rather, the human

being is inevitably drawn into long-term activities that require enduring commitment, as well as special focus, attention, and energy, and
sometimes, developed expertise. Human beings do not just act: they
are office workers, farmers, mail clerks, parents. This specificity is a
very widespread crosscultural and even transepochal phenomenon,
and is as true of hunters and gatherers of Stone Age culture as it is of
professionals in a technocratic society. All have *primary occupations*
that require different kinds of activities and, as constituting enduring
life situations, have distinctive dimensions. Moreover, to employ a
distinction of Hannah Arendt's, a primary occupation can be either
labor or work or a mixture of the two.[8] Living in the world in the mode
of faith does not eliminate the life situation constituted by one's primary occupation. As yet another corruptible and redeemable situation,
the life situation constituted by one's work poses an enduring challenge
to reflective interpretation. Work theologically interpreted and experienced in faith is *vocation*.[9] Vocation thus calls forth and presupposes a
distinctive type of interpretation or hermeneutic mode. It constitutes
an enduring life situation to be interpreted, in which occur specific
situations, activities, and responsibilities that evoke interpretation.
Like the other elemental types of interpretation, interpretation centered in the idea of people's vocations has not been utterly absent from
the church's education. But because the study of theology has come to
be restricted to clergy education, vocation—or work interpreted theologically—has suffered a concomitant restriction to just one primary
occupation, that of the clergy. Accordingly, as a general and elemental
type of interpretation, interpretation that is centered in the idea of
vocation has been excluded from the structure of theological study and,
therefore, from church education.

Thus, five elemental types of interpretation are called forth by the
existence of faith in life situations. The most comprehensive type of
interpretation is that in which the other elemental types distinctive of
faith come together in concrete acts. A second elemental type is
subordinate to the first: it is the kind of interpretation called forth by
one sort of particularly consequential life situation—the life situation
constituted by one's work. The other three elemental types reflect the
distinctive dimensions that enter life situations because of faith: the
dimensions of tradition, of the truth of the gospel, and of praxis. The
dimensions behind all five elemental types of interpretation have Latin

names: *mundus, vocatio, traditio, veritas,* and *actio.* These determine the basic hermeneutic modes, which education brings to self-consciousness, rigorization, and discipline.

Mapping the Terrain

Education, in the sense of ordered learning, should not be restricted to higher learning and higher education. It can occur from grade school on. Equally, the rigorization and disciplining of faith's reflective interpretation can begin as early as ordered learning can begin.[10] Theological study can occur in a variety of environments (in congregations, clergy schools, universities) and among all age groups. Whatever the environment, the study should be shaped by all five elemental modes of interpretation. If, for example, the disciplining through ordered learning proceeded without reference to the church's specific mythos and tradition, it would neglect a basic dimension of the believer's situation. That would not mean that tradition was actually eliminated from the situation. As a dimension it is intrinsic to it. It would mean that ordered learning offered no disciplining assistance to the interpretation of tradition. Thus the five elemental types of interpretation establish a measure for how adequately any instance of theological ordered learning offers resources for the disciplining of faith's reflective life.

It is important to distinguish between the *aims* and the *subject matter* or *content* of education. The aims of an educative effort answer the following question. What will the course of study do to fulfill the needs or agendas projected for or by those who take it? If we ask about the aims of a cooking course, the answer is not given by simply mentioning cuisine, which is the course's subject matter. Nor are the aims of theological study stated by mentioning subject matters such as the gospel, the church, the Christian faith, or the ministry. Aims are expressed in the grammar of infinitives and the language of purpose: *to* communicate information about, *to* facilitate skill in. Theological study can aim *to* form the student spiritually, *to* create scholars, *to* train or sharpen church-leadership (ministry) skills, *to* inform the student about the gospel and the church's tradition. It is the aims of a pedagogical undertaking that determine what contents or subject matters are and are not included in it. A theological school whose sole aim is to teach clergy skills will develop a curriculum very different from that of a school whose aim is to prepare scholars. Educational programs that arrange theological study according to subject matter but without articulated aims remain without real basis. They evoke the following question: In the light of what aims are you proposing this content of study and not another?

A major argument of this book is that the aim of theological study, as *theological*, is not to teach clergy skills, provide spiritual formation, or mold scholars but to communicate and discipline basic modes of interpretation already at work in the believer's situation. The five hermeneutic modes do not enforce a specific curriculum but disclose the *aims* of the course of study. They provide us with certain guiding criteria but do not dictate the structure of the study itself. We face now the problem toward which the two essays have been moving. Given these aims or guiding criteria, how do we discern a *pedagogical* structure? How do we get from the hermeneutic modes of the situation of the believer to the requisites for a course of study?

I do not think it is possible logically to derive a pedagogical structure from these requisites or criteria. The aims of a school's program of studies always reflect the specific situation and context of the school.[11] In addition, any subject matter will set requirements of pedagogy that do not flow simply from the aims of study. After all, world history must talk about epochs (ancient, modern) and regions (Eastern, Western, American) not because of the aims of historical study but because of the very nature of world history.

How do the aims of theological study and its subject matter function together to create a pattern of study? Schleiermacher's *Brief Outline of Theological Study* illustrates the tension created when an attempt is made to take both aims and subject matter into consideration. Schleiermacher offered a pattern of theological study that was meant to serve the aim of study (the training of the leadership of the church) at the same time that it did justice to the subject matter (Christianity, especially in its "essence").[12] His proposed threefold pattern of study was the result. I have contended that there are modes of interpretation conforming to the fundamental dimensions of the believer's redemptive existence in the world. These dimensions are not simply something "subjective," at the consciousness pole, although the emphasis is certainly on the believer rather than an object or content. But another emphasis is possible which focuses not on the believer but on the condition, reality, or reference of redemptive existence. Are we talking here about God and the Word of God? Still, God is never an unmediated content. God is active, "revealed," and the subject of discourse only in the historical mediation of a specific faith—in this case, the Christian faith, the ecclesial community, the Christian religion, the church.[13] I therefore think that Schleiermacher is right in his way of conceiving the larger referent or subject matter of theological study. The objective reality of redemptive existence in the world, in the sense of its necessary context and condition, is the Christian faith. The Christian faith is consequently the most general subject matter, the content, of theological study.[14] It is just that Schleiermacher's description of the aim of theological study is too narrow. It reduces the theological sciences to the "positive science" of clergy education. But though I characterize the aim of theological study more broadly than Schleiermacher does—as the disciplining of the basic modes of interpretation that occur in the situation of faith—I agree with him that the subject matter of theological study is the total complex of historical, ontological, personal, and communitarian realities that come together as the Christian faith.

A curriculum—that is, a course of study—is in the most superficial sense a pattern of courses distributed into pedagogical areas. In this pattern are two deeper structures. The first is the pattern viewed as a movement, an order of courses which requires a beginning and moves to an end. The second is the distribution of expertise and scholarship required as resources for pedagogy and inquiry. Students experience a curriculum primarily as a movement, faculty as a map of the areas of expertise. Curriculum, therefore, looks one way when described in its movement, another way in its distribution of scholarly specialties. What follows is an attempt to see how the movement of a program of theological study can incorporate the basic modes of interpretation.

Foundational Studies

When considering an educational program not as a map of sciences but as a movement of studies, we need to resist the temptation to see the movement as linear travel through the existing disciplines. The task is not just that of deciding which disciplines go first, which second, and so forth. Decisions much more radical than that must be made. One of the very first is whether theological study requires at ground level a set of studies that can serve as a support and presupposition for everything else. In the theological faculties of nineteenth-century Germany, there was an initiatory course, namely theological encyclopedia, that introduced the student to the rationale and panorama of theology, and that vindicated the fourfold pattern of theological studies, in which the student moved from biblical studies to church history to systematics to practical studies. If theological education is a disciplining of basic hermeneutic modes, that is, of types of interpretation and understanding, are there studies which create foundations for this?[15]

Any proposal about foundational studies will inevitably reflect the specific situation of a particular school, including its context, aims, educational level, and the like. But even when the programs of study occur in very different institutions (e.g., in institutions with congregational education and those with clergy education as their ends), certain types of study are called for which initiate the study of theology.[16] A program of theological study is better conceived if it does not begin directly with the disciplining of the modes of interpretation but, rather, first acquaints the student with what that disciplining itself presupposes.[17] There are areas of knowledge and cognitive postures that the student needs in order to interpret tradition and action. Three stand out as important foundational requisites to any program of theological study structured by elemental hermeneutic modes.

One of the elemental modes of interpretation is at the same time both the most inclusive and the most specific. It is the interpretation of situations. But a program of study is itself a situation. Coming together in that situation are the institution of study, the students' biographical situations, the branch or denomination of a religious faith, the power structure of the social world (administrative, racial, sexual, political, class-oriented). Feminists are today calling for men to recognize that what they have accomplished and what they continue to do are made possible by their privileged position in society and in the churches and the schools. It seems clear that education that focuses on modes of understanding and interpretation is skewed when there is an obliviousness about the social context in which the education takes place. Hence, among the foundational studies for students of theology belong those whose aim is to articulate the comprehensive concrete cultural context and situation of religion and the church. These studies would call attention to the fact that human beings as such and as believers exist in situations whose complexity, relativity, and corruptness call for intense awareness. Included in these studies would be a focus on the present situation of the church and religion.

The second agenda for foundational studies has likewise to do with identifying postures and approaches that can skew theological study from the start. It too encompasses a set of studies that help raise the interpreting consciousness and that anticipate studies in interpretive modes. This is what Schleiermacher called philosophical theology, and Karl Rahner the "transcendental" aspect of theological study. Francis Fiorenza calls it fundamental theology.[18]

Interpretations of tradition and basic historiographical postures contain paradigms, even ontologies, of individual and social human being. Paradigms of some sort are operative in all historical epochs and in every cultural ethos. Even the "culture of professionalism" appearing in theological schools, which takes ministers to be professionals with largely managerial and therapeutic roles, embodies a philosophical anthropology. Clergy vocational studies—for instance, pastoral psychology, church administration, and homiletics—are guided by paradigms of reality. Explicitly or tacitly these movements make presuppositions about language, power, tragic being, and sociality. In addition, all the elemental modes of interpretation are affected by convictions about these matters. Whether the human being is conceived as a quantifiable entity and the passive receptacle of various causalities or as a self-transcending person existing in a distinctive way in relation to others will shape the way action, truth and reality, vocation, and the historic process (traditioning) will be approached, defined, and interpreted.

The themes of human being and the human condition, the themes of "anthropology," are foundational to theological studies. Human being is not simply one theme of the liberal arts among many or one locus of doctrine beside others. For, first, the movement of theological study must begin and not just end with some self-consciousness about what it is buying into when it appropriates the myths and paradigms through which the larger culture interprets human realities, whether they are the paradigms of therapeutics, technical reason, or biological reductionism. The powerful and frequently corrupting effect of these paradigms on human thinking and being calls for their identification and critical assessment. Here, the criticism of culture functions also as theology's self-criticism. Second, all of the modes of interpretation occur in the situation of redemptive existence in the world. The movement of theological study is not from theory or authority to "applications." It is a movement that permits the elemental modes of interpretation to be identified and disciplined. Theological study in the basic modes of interpretation *is* a kind of anthropology, a paradigm of human being and the human condition. However central revelation, grace, and theonomy are to this paradigm, they are not mere heteronomous destructions or displacements of human reality. To make them so is to resign human being in its embodiment, lived time and lived space, linguistically, historicity, and social being to the prevailing and corrupted cultural paradigms. Redemptive existence becomes, then, a compartment, a sphere of "spirituality" occurring out of relation to what the human being is in its created being. When clergy education suppresses the anthropology of human being by marginalizing it into an idiosyncratic specialty, it risks trivialization.

I am contending here for a theological account of human reality and the human condition as part of foundational studies. I am not, however, urging that theological studies start with "natural theology." We are not confronted with a choice between revelation (Christocentricity, grace, faith) and ontology. It is just that theological study cannot proceed from propaedeutic studies directly to the hermeneutic modes without critically confronting the paradigms of human being that are already in the air it breathes, and without understanding in at least a preliminary way the human reality that all the modes of interpretation pertain to.

The third portion of the foundational studies I am commending would promote some knowledge of Christianity as a historical reality, since that historical reality is the presupposition of all the modes of theological interpretation. Here too we have the subject matter that is present in the three primary types of understanding and interpretation correlative to the dimensions of faith. In theological study one learns to interpret the tradition's memory of the Christian faith, the believer's truth assessment of the faith, and the action prompted by the Christian faith. There is a difference, however, between the way the Christian faith as a subject matter is taken up in the foundational studies and how it continues to be studied after that. As the focus of an initiating study the historical phenomenon of the Christian faith must be viewed comprehensively. What is needed at the foundational stage is a panorama of that multidimensional phenomenon—not just a treatment of the subject such as one finds in the period specialties of church history. Postfoundational studies of the Christian faith build on this, continue it, but always press the question of the distinctiveness of this faith.[19]

The Primary Hermeneutic Modes

The initial movement in the study of theology is, thus, from foundational studies to the modes of interpretation. If these modes are to be disciplined, they must become the subject of inquiry and teaching in the course of study. In addition, theological study has a movement because some of the modes of interpretation are logically prior to others. Although all the modes influence the way any one of them is pursued even when abstracted, two of the elemental modes are syntheses of reflection in which the other three elemental modes cohere. The two concern the interpretation of situations and, as a special instance of that, interpretation that is centered in the concept of vocation, that is, of the work constituting one's primary occupation. Thus, when the believer interprets a situation—for instance, one related to nuclear disarmament or a drug problem in the family—the interpretation is shaped and guided by the symbols, "truths," and narratives of the tradition of the community of faith. When church leaders take up their specific responsibilities—for instance, preaching or administration—they too are interpreting situations, and the other four modes coalesce in their interpretive activities.

The interpretation of tradition. One of the foundational studies targets the subject matter of theological study, the Christian faith. As a historical reality the Christian faith is mediated through a community's activity of transmitting a living tradition and through linguistic sedimentations and the survival of social institutions from the past. The foundational studies of the Christian faith cannot be thought of as ending when studies in the hermeneutic modes begin. Understanding the Christian faith is a lifelong task for the interpreting believer. But that task entails not simply the accumulation of information about a panoramic historical reality but also an understanding of the distinctive claim embodied in the reality's events, narratives, imagery, and doctrines. And for that there are required many interpretative studies.

Does the Christian faith manifest not only a sedimented tradition but a distinctive activity of transmitting and reshaping tradition that itself calls for interpretation? What place does the faith of Israel and Judaism have in the community's transmission of tradition? Questions like these show that the study of the Christian faith does not end with the foundational studies. Instead, the initial panoramic study of the Christian faith creates the basis for retrieval-oriented study of that faith as tradition.

The Christian faith, as a complex historical reality, has dimensions: temporal, institutional, moral, intersubjective, linguistic. One's understanding of the Christian faith will not necessarily be advanced by shopping from a school's list of electives in the field of church history. That tends to be what the student must do when the offered courses reflect the "expertise curriculum," the hegemony of specialty fields. The student takes a denominational history, a course in early American religious history, a seminar in Augustine, and a survey course in the free-church tradition of the Reformation. A mélange of this sort will do something: it will give certain historical information as well as acquaint the student with certain historiographic methods. It would be rare that such an aggregate of courses would facilitate much awareness of the interpretation of tradition as a hermeneutic mode. One reason is that the Christian faith as a historical phenomenon is not simply a miscellany of abstracted figures and epochs but a movement that is rooted in ancient Israel, has originating events, periods of classical formation and reformation (Catholic and Protestant), and periods of breakup and of challenge to its classical historical forms.

Historical understanding involves grasping continuities and differentiations over time. In addition, it requires grasping the dimensional complexity of the historical phenomenon. And though the panoramic history of foundational studies may communicate something of this dimensionality, the emphasis there is on transmitting a basic knowledge of the comprehensive reality of the Christian faith, not on interpreting the Christian faith as a tradition. A minimum condition for the exercise of the hermeneutic mode of tradition is knowledge of the historical movement of the Christian faith, from its origins, to its classical forms and its postclassical fate.[20] It is difficult to imagine a theological struggle with action or truth and reality which proceeds directly from a series of historical facts about Christianity but without a sense of its historical movement or its dimensionality. In addition, the interpretation of tradition requires an awareness of how the dimensions of the Christian faith affect its interpretation. Thus, to interpret the Christian faith, to understand what it is, involves a grasp of the historic process and the distinctive traditioning of ecclesial existence, the operations of power, and the role of comprehensive visions (ideas, mythoi) in traditioning.[21] The study of tradition as an abstractable mode of interpretation builds on the presentation of the historical movement and dimensionality of the Christian faith from its beginning to modernity.

The interpretation of truth. To make a case for the question of truth as intrinsic to the structure of theological study is to face a formidable task. The cards of this game are very much stacked. I have contended that religious faiths as such set claims of truth and reality and any serious interpretation of the faiths as faiths must respond to and assess their claims. Further, I argued that the believer is disposed toward the tradition as a bearer of truth and reality, not of fiction or deception.[22] But however well grounded my conclusions might be, they may be less than persuasive when applied to actual courses of theological study. I think it is not too much of an exaggeration to say that the question about the truth of the faith is marginal for most programs of study in current clergy education. Even though specific courses take up that question, it has little impact on the way the movement of theological study is conceived. What marginalizes the truth question is a contemporary form of the precritical distortion of thought that conflates the settling of truth with the interpretation of an authoritative text, for instance, Scripture. Even when historical-critical modes of thought are acknowledged, the legacy continues in the formulation of the movement of theological study as proceeding from the exegetically interpreted text to applications. When this theory-to-practice legacy disintegrates, the two curricular moments of tradition (Scripture) and practical theology separate into independent specialty fields. And when that happens, the truth question divides into establishing the exegesis as historically accurate and establishing relevant applications. Truth, then, becomes either an immanent content of the text uncovered by some new and clever hermeneutic, or relevant application. Recent approaches to clergy education as a technology of clergy skills draw on and exacerbate this approach and its repression of the truth question. Insofar as theological study is seen as this text-to-practice movement, the question of the truth of things is relegated to a curricular idiosyncrasy, something pursued by students with a "philosophical" aptitude and by certain faculty specialists. The repression and marginalization of the truth question are not just phenomena of clergy education. A therapeutic society reduces the passionate eros for knowledge to a pursuit of data and to information retrieval and the management of individual and social outcomes.[23]

The therapeutic-managerial mentality and the legacy of authority-to-application may be sufficiently powerful to maintain this repression. But to the degree that the church, its schools, and the university acknowledge historical and critical modes of thought, they cannot identify the interpretive description of the classic texts, however classic they are, with a search for truth and manifest reality. The truth of the claims embodied in historical bearers (epochs, figures, institution, texts) must always be otherwise established if it is to be intellectually responsible to accept them. For some the truth is established only by reference to realities manifest in and intrinsic to the community of faith and the experience of faith (fideism). For others it is established by criteria and references outside the circle of faith (transcendental, natural, and correlational theology). In either case, the acknowledgment of the historicality of classic texts calls into existence a struggle with truth and reality which is distinct from the exposition of historical contents. In my judgment this distinction is already latent in the situation of the believer, and the conflation of truth with texts violates the structure of that situation.

What is required for a disciplining of the mode of interpretation having to do with truth and reality? We would misformulate this question if we construed it as an invitation to decide between philosophically competing theories of truth, one of which we select as appropriate to theology. In my view the philosophical theories (correspondence, coherence, unconcealment) supplement rather than exclude one another. One thing I think necessary is, instead, attention to certain formal features that seem to be perennially present when we struggle with the truth of things in any of the senses of truth. There are formal issues about what is occurring in the interpretation of something as true, and any course of study that seeks to discipline this mode of interpretation has to attend to those issues.

Still, a metahermeneutic of truth cannot be the central task of the study of this mode of interpretation. For the truth question is not just a formal question. It is chiefly a question about whether the claims of faith are true and about whether our world is illumined by those claims. A claim of faith is not so much a hypothesis or a proposition as an attested mystery. The historical movement of tradition contains many interpretations of this mystery which must be assessed for their truth. Although the truth question is at the center of this primary mode of interpretation, it is present in some form in all the elemental modes. When a preoccupation with the truth of things guides historical exposition, exposition presses beneath summary accounts to the strata of presuppositions that are uncovered only when one thinks along with the text in its own canvass of the truth. Similarly, no hermeneutic of situations, practical actions, or vocations occurs without making use of the truth of tradition or without attempting to uncover the living truth of these things.

Contrariwise, the other modes of interpretation also contribute to this one. Both situationality and action contribute to what we mean by truth. Nor is anything "true" which is not mediated in some way through the historic process and its paradigms.

I have used the terms "truth" and "reality" in a way that avoids construing the truth question as one simply of logic—of demonstration, induction, and the like. The truth of things is also the reality of things. Nor can the truth of faith be formulated in utter indifference to world structures and processes, to the nature and operations of history, to the being of human beings. To the degree that this is forgotten, theological study occurs as a cognitive enclave among the sciences, appropriating only the sciences that assist its theory (text history) or its applications—in other words, the historical and social sciences. Theology since Kant has found biblicist and transcendental reasons for shuffling off the burden of "metaphysics" and "physicotheology." The result is the virtual indifference of contemporary theology to the sciences that mark off areas of our world for study and to the world picture now being produced in microbiology, physics, and astronomy.[24] The disrelation or nonrelation of the world of faith to the structures of creation effects a certain "unreality" in the former and in the environments that interpret it. Faith's relations to the world thus constitute an important dimension for the interpretation of the truth and reality of faith and, therefore, for theological study.

The interpretation of action. Action is a dimension of the believer's situation irreducible to its other dimensions.[25] Is it sufficiently important and, potentially, sufficiently discrete to be abstracted into a pedagogical area of theological study? It can be argued that interpreting action is simply a responsible way of interpreting situations. It can also be argued, as it has been by some liberation theologians, that truth and reality are synonymous with action and that the question of truth *is* the question of action. I think both views are correct in affirming that human beings cannot exist in situations or grasp what is real apart from action. But whether action can be abstracted as a pedagogical moment depends on the degree to which it is a distinctive way of existing in a situation and toward reality. Action and situationality are not synonymous. Action is existing in a situation so as to bring about an outcome that is guided by a certain agenda. Grocery shopping is an action, and so is demonstrating against apartheid. Action, therefore, has an element of *futurity* (toward the prospective outcome) and an element of *responsibility* (toward that in behalf of which the agenda is ordered). The question of action, then, is how to exist responsibly in a situation with certain outcomes in view. This can be a social as well as an individual question. Because existence includes both acting and being in situations, the issue of action includes issues of virtue as well as of policies and strategies. When action is the reference of an act of interpretation, there is a look toward something projected. The focus of the interpretation is *future, possible, preferential action*—responsible existence oriented to effect outcomes in a situation. Because of the element of responsibility, and therefore of preference and norm, to exist in a situation in the mode of action is also to transcend the situation. That is, it is existence that is distanced from the situation by the project of effecting an outcome not identical to the situation. Action surpasses and transcends the situation by projecting an altered situation. Action, then, is an assessive and altering way of existing in a situation. And while it is proper to say with the liberation theologians that action is a dimension of reality, the reality question is broader than simply the question of prospective preferential action.

What is it to make action the subject of a pedagogical area of theological study? Action is already a subject matter of clergy education in the specialty fields (ethics, clergy-oriented practical theology) and in action-oriented movements and their literatures—black, feminist, and liberation. Yet these are thematizings of action which rarely come together in a pedagogy of action itself as a hermeneutic mode. Instead, we have expositions of the literatures of praxis and liberation; various types of ethics, which together do not add up to a mode of interpretation; and various courses on the professional activities of clergy. The effect of this curricular arrangement is to play down the mode of interpretation that centers upon action and so completely to split its subject matter into specialty fields that the intrinsic relation between this mode of interpretation and the modes of tradition, truth and reality, and situations is masked.

Like the pedagogy concerning truth and reality, the teaching of action covers both the delineation of formal features of the interpretation of action and themes that occur when faith and action come together. The formal pedagogy of action attends to the constitutive features of the situation of action and of its interpretation. The subject of this pedagogy is future, possible, preferred action, corporate and individual. The pedagogy of action should bring about a distinctive hermeneutic awareness and skill directed toward the special requirements that action places on the interpreter. Formal philosophy and theology of action attends to both social and individual features of interpretive situations like those of desire, decision, planning, policy, change, power, maintenance, and instrumentality. These features embrace both individual and social agency. The theological hermeneutic of action also studies, in its formal role, the way these features occur in the situation of faith, which means how they are brought into relation to tradition, Scripture, norms and criteria, the ecclesial community, human corruption, and redemptive existence.

But a theological pedagogy of action clearly addresses more than just formal and methodological considerations. The reason is that action itself, the preferential and responsible effecting of outcomes, is something evoked by very specific predicaments and contexts—often by peril, pain, tragic ambiguity, catastrophe, and crisis. Accordingly, the pedagogy of action can never be abstracted from the situations that call for action—situations facing schools, nations, the world, nature, the social world, one's family, and so forth. It would be both premature and arbitrary to propose a way of organizing the pedagogical area of action. I do think that the interpretation of action would fare better if several kinds of action interpretation now current in clergy education could be brought together into one area—for instance, feminist, black, and liberation theologies, "ethics," "spirituality," liturgy, and sacraments.[26] Liberation theologies articulate the action dimension of theology. They correct any theological reflection that forgets that dimension, and they thus contribute an action-oriented hermeneutic or mode of interpretation.

Liturgics and sacramental theology are themes of ecclesiology, but ecclesiology presides over all the modes of interpretation as the communal pole of faith. What is more, the church's liturgy and sacraments must not be thought to be mere instrumentalities of clergy "practical theology," since they form a dimension of the *vita activa* of lay believers and their communities as well.

Action should not be reduced to activity. Outcomes are not only events but also states and modes of existing. A revolution and what follows can be an outcome but so can a formed pattern of virtues. Consequently, action can hold in view all kinds of desiderata: social and individual, active and passive, transitory and enduring. It follows that the nonformal part of the pedagogy of action must take up individual redemptive existence, social redemptive existence, the action of social entities (communities, institutions), and the major issues of the current context (nation-state militarism, the threat to the ecology of the planet, prison reform). These areas may be sufficiently distinct to require differentiated research and teaching, that is, their own theological study, but the study should never be so compartmentalized as to obscure action as a distinct mode of interpretation.

The Synthetic Hermeneutic Modes

Theological study is primarily a movement from studies in Christian faith to studies in the elemental, abstractable modes of interpretation. Within these modes themselves, however, there must also be movement, since two of the modes require a synthesis of, and so follow upon, the other three—tradition, truth and reality, and action.

Situational hermeneutics. The most comprehensive kind of human

interpretation is the interpretation of an inclusive situation. The term
"situation" is not common parlance in the literature of theological
study. Used frequently in this volume, it does not lend itself to common-sense definition, even though it expresses a reality of everyday
life. Succinctly expressed, a situation is a temporal-spatial configuration
of the life world. "Life world" names the surrounding world as it is
experienced. This is not the world in the sense of the cosmos. It is
closer to the kind of world that is meant in references to the world of
high fashion or the world of academia. Going to college, taking a new
job, or visiting another country on vacation all involve different life
worlds. Briefer and more regional situations can occur within those that
are more enduring and more inclusive. As something enduring and
spatial, a situation has its own distinctive features, which are not so
much "objects" as dimensions of realities. Attending a theater is a
situation with a particular past, a specific physical setting, a set of
expectations and attitudes on the part of the participant (aesthetic,
sexual, leisure-time), a structure of social power and influence, and a
way of being together with other human beings. Complex as this brief
and local situation is, it is uncomplicated compared with the global
situation of large nation-states struggling to obtain power and influence
in the Third World.

Teaching that focuses on situations does occur in clergy education,
but, as with the teaching that has action as its subject matter, in such a
compartmentalized way that a pedagogy of this hermeneutic mode
never comes into existence. It is evident that the interpretation of
situations is constitutive of the situation of the believer. Can this mode
of interpretation be taught? The other modes are subject to pedagogy
because they are directed to dimensions of reality that can be abstracted into fairly well demarcated entities. To qualify as something to
be taught, the situational mode of interpretation must have identifiable
and recurring features. When we interpret situations, there is a certain
inattention or obliviousness to what we are doing. If the features of our
situational interpretations can be recovered, a pedagogy of situations
can be a part of the structure of theological study in two ways: there can
be a formal teaching of the features of this mode of interpretation, and
there can be the interpretation of characteristic situations of action,
vocation, world crisis, and the like.

It is important to note the distinctive agenda of this moment of theological study. The theological interpretation of situations has descriptive rather than normative aims. Undisciplined interpretation tends to respond to things in immediate assessive judgments. A moralizing response to a friend's impending divorce blanks out an important step, namely, that of ascertaining the situation in its complexity. Even when a remissive element softens the moralizing response, it may still be a response to a falsely construed or vastly oversimplified state of affairs. Theory-to-practice clergy education has reinforced the natural tendency to judge before understanding, for when the important thing is thought to be the bringing to bear of some authority upon the realities of the world, the exact and manifold details of those realities and of the situations in which they figure in our life world fade correspondingly in perceived importance. It is possible to multiply examples of responses that "apply" the authoritative tradition in direct acts of assessment without the disciplined act of ascertaining the realities of the assessed situation. Frequently the situation is obscured by exclusive attention to a person, an entity, or an aspect within it. Thus, most of the complexities in the situation of impending divorce are ignored by a response that leaps directly to the guilt of one party. There are, of course, pedagogical areas in clergy education that attend to some types of situational complexity. Having appropriated the psychological and social sciences, they attend to psycho- or sociogenetic dimensions. Still lacking, however, is a thematization of situational interpretation as such. For situational interpretation is broader than the appropriation of the conceptual framework of a specific science, for instance, psychology. Constituting the believer's responses to things is interpretation in the sense of a self-conscious and disciplined reading of the complexity and dimensionality of what is interpreted.

The educative disciplining of the interpretation of situations is in part a formal, perhaps even an ontological, undertaking. At the same time, it must also attend to selected concrete situations constituting the ongoing context or life world of the believer, church, school, and society. In this respect, the pedagogical area might, following an older nomenclature, be called the theology of culture. But that would be acceptable only if "culture" referred to the inclusive and current situation to which theological reflection is directed. Does this mean that current clergy education covers the area adequately, with its miscellany of courses in the field? It is crucial to keep in mind that the inclusive current situation is never a mere mélange of themes but is constituted by enduring problematic situations. There are, of course, no fixed number of such problematic situations, and any one person's list will be idiosyncratic. For illustrative purposes, I would suggest three culture-determining situations that are at present of critical importance for the believer and the church. All three call for disciplined hermeneutic description. Each one is so prominent in the current cultural situation that its omission from theological study would give the study the character of provincial isolation, ideology, and the legitimation of oppressive power. I shall refer to the three as the situation of world faiths, the situation of power and politics, and the situation of the church. All three constitute the world in which the believer and the community of faith exist and to which they interpretively respond. These three situations may or may not mark off disciplines. They are mentioned rather as focuses of important areas in the pedagogy of situations or culture.

Some study of *world faiths* was at one time fairly widespread in clergy education. The impetus toward such study was provided by the nineteenth-century missionary movement; hence, the framework and motives prompting the study were conversionist. Seminaries have seen a decline in the study of world faiths since that time, resulting in a new isolation and religious provincialism exactly when world faiths are more and more forced to acknowledge one another. To the extent that clergy education is guided by a narrow professional model, it will tend to reduce the ambit of its interest to the specific social reality of the denomination, since that is the arena in which professional responsibilities will be discharged. A further reduction centers the curriculum on preparing the student for professional functions in congregations. These reductions result in a virtual denial of reality, because they project a contextless denomination and contextless congregations.

Two circumstances prompt contemporary theological study—clergy, lay, or university—to include a comparative hermeneutic of world faiths.[27] First, the situation of the believer and the church is now constituted by configurations that reach all the way to global situations. Religion constitutes one important part of the global situation and of the encounter and conflict of culture and nation-states. Second, critical orientations have modified the conversionist attitude toward other world faiths. It is not that the several religious faiths have no distinctive wisdom to offer, and no distinctive attestation to make to the truth of things. It is rather that there must be a mutual recognition of their respective truths.[28] Hence, part of the current situation of the believer is the religious "other" as the bearer of a determinate wisdom. This interhuman situation modifies how all the specific faiths are present one to another, not by calling into question the integrity, distinctiveness, or reality carried by each faith but by creating a new way of being a determinate and specific faith. This new specificity is that of codetermination, of being with other modes of faith. We can devise curricula that ignore or even impede codetermination, but the nearness of alternative faith structures is an inescapable part of the current global situation.

Power also calls for a descriptive hermeneutic. We could equally say *politics*. The situation of power and politics is that in which human beings come together to establish and maintain social controls of various sorts. The scope of this situation is enormous, running from the global village, with its interdependent economic and military systems calling for planetwide ecological analysis, to familial and congregational systems.[29] It includes infrastructures and the systemic evil of oppression and ideology. A hermeneutic of the political would require attention to the constitutive being-together, the intersubjectivity, of human beings; the structure of social maintenance; the formation of primary symbols; the way language serves power; and much more. In clergy education, courses in feminism, church management, ethics, and black studies take up these themes. But courses like these presuppose and call for an explicit hermeneutic of power, a pedagogy that attends to what constitutes situations of this type.

The third pervasive situation that can focus the pedagogy of situation or culture is that of *the church*, the community of faith. The church operates at many social levels: as a branch of Christendom (the situation of world Catholicism), as a denomination (the situation of the Southern Baptists), as a denominational bureaucracy, as a congregation, as a heterodox movement, and so forth. Moreover, Christianity as a world faith exists in a global situation. Within the Christian religion, many branches and denominations participate in the ecumenical movement. Efforts are now under way to ascertain the causes of the apparent decline of North American mainline Protestant denominations. Although these matters set special tasks for the leadership of the churches, they also engage all believers as elements of their churchly situation. Hence, the church's situation is intrinsic to theological study as such.

The hermeneutic of vocation. In the clerical paradigm, theological study *means* studies for and by the professional leadership of the church. In this setting, vocation is considered to pertain only to the called leadership. I suggested earlier, however, that vocation occurs as believers respond in faith to their primary occupations. On this view the hermeneutic of vocation is not simply clergy hermeneutics, and its disciplining pedagogy cannot be restricted to clergy or seminary studies. The matter of clergy education aside, a hermeneutic of vocation for the believer or the university student of the Christian religion must seek to understand both the primary and the secondary situations of vocation.

The primary situation of vocation is the work forming the primary occupation of the human being. To believe this is not necessarily to surrender to an older piety that seeks work-sanctioning "calls" to particular occupations—to nursing, farm labor, plumbing, or heavy-metal music. To suppose that there are "calls" in this sense invites human beings self-deceptively to invent specific divine sanctions for what they do. A similar self-deception occurs when church leaders imagine that there are specific callings to their line of work alone. Rather, the point is that the believer need not live in a dichotomy that severs work from the spiritual and churchly life. The environments or social worlds of work in contemporary society pose special problems of interpretation. The environments may be governmental, military, educational or corporate bureaucracies, small shops or stores, or service-oriented institutions. Almost all of them are organized around the successful accumulation of the primary means of survival, power, and influence—namely, money. Work involves specific kinds of social relations, opportunities for human accomplishment, and occasions in which there is the corrupt experience of power. It is through work and the primary occupation that culture exercises its most powerful influence on human beings. If believers regard work as outside the sphere of theological interpretation, they turn the issues associated with work and the environments of work over to the environments of work themselves. They subjugate themselves to the management of human responses that the work environments promote. This is why work poses a special hermeneutic task for theological study which is not reducible to clergy education.[30]

In addition to the primary situation of vocation, there is for the believer a secondary situation as well: that of the believer's "occupation" in the ecclesial community. The community of faith is the occasion of egalitarian experience in the sharing of ritual, sacramental life, worship, and social life. But the community of faith cannot, ironically enough, nurture this egalitarian experience without allocating tasks and responsibilities. An utterly hierarchical allocation loads virtually all the tasks onto the ordained leadership—which in the past was, and in some quarters still is, wholly male. In a nonhierarchical allocation, the community of faith endures over time and pursues its aims through a wider distribution of roles and responsibilities: of teaching, music, community service, pastoral care. The responsibilities may be brief (e.g., a stint of official leadership) or enduring (e.g., a lifelong teaching of children). In any case, they do not constitute one's primary occupation or work. They instead define special situations that evoke the believer's interpretive responses. Vocation, then, embraces both the believer's work and the believer's special way of being part of the ecclesial community. Both are situations of interpretation and both call for disciplining—that is, self-conscious rigorization—of the interpretation by ordered learning.

Clergy education, now a postbaccalaureate three- or four-year professional program, is not identical with theological education but is a special instance of it. As an intrinsic hermeneutic dimension of all theological study, vocation is not unique to clergy education. But in clergy education the work of the primary occupation is itself an occupation in the community of faith. Because of this coalescence of the work vocation and the ecclesial vocation, vocation can form a basis of unity for clergy education.[31] Things go wrong only when clergy education takes vocation to be the subject matter of its study or to be an aim that excludes the other modes of interpretation. On my view, vocation is a part of the believer's situation. Accordingly, it sets the task of a distinctive mode of interpretation and a pedagogy that disciplines that interpretation. But *all* of the elemental interpretive modes must collaborate in disciplining the reflective interpretations of the ordained leader and in developing the leader's required skills. Clergy education is distinctive in that it calls for an ordered learning that points toward church leadership as work. It is not distinctive in the sense of occurring outside the structure of theological study or of dispensing with the basic modes of interpretation. Hence, weakened and corrupted programs of theological study are produced when clergy education attends only to tradition and vocation at the expense of the other dimensions of faith's situation.

NOTES

1. The broadening of hermeneutics is a major event in the intellectual West. Generally described, a shift occurs from hermeneutics as an effort to retrieve texts for practice to hermeneutics as a philosophical theory of human understanding. See Roy J. Howard, *Three Faces of Hermeneutics: An Introduction to Current Theories of Understanding* (Berkeley and Los Angeles: Univ. of California Press, 1982), pref. For a survey of this broadening, see Josef Bleicher, *Contemporary Hermeneutics: Hermeneutic as Method, Philosophy, and Critique* (Boston and London: Routledge & Kegan Paul, 1980). Bleicher traces the hermeneutic movement from its classical origin in the romantic movement and in nineteenth-century historiography, to its passage through the sort of social science that was conceived as a science of historical spirit *(Geisteswissenschaft)* and through philosophy by way of Heidegger and Hans Georg Gadamer and the critical-social philosophy of the Frankfurt school, and finally to the new directions of Paul Ricoeur. The broadening of hermeneutics has already occurred in Wilhelm Dilthey, who sees the problem as one about the nature of understanding and not just the retrieval of texts. Texts themselves require a grasp of *frender-Seelenzustande*, "states of affairs of the other consciousness" ("Die Entstehung der Hermeneutik" [1900], in *Gesammelte-Schriften*, vol. 5). A decisive broadening occurs when Gadamer, drawing on Heidegger, sees hermeneutics as a description of the "mode of the whole human experience of the world." His contention is that when we attempt this description, what we find is an already-interpreted world *(Philosophical Hermeneutics* [Berkeley and Los Angeles: Univ. of California Press, 1976], 15). Richard Rorty traces the development of modern hermeneutics out of Nietzsche's revolt against Platonism and his abandonment of the pursuit of a science of immediately given realities in favor of the more modest task of interrogating human interpretive orientations. Once the broadening occurred, disputes arose over focus—for instance, between the hermeneutic of tradition (Gadamer) and ideology criticism (Jürgen Habermas, Karl Apel). For this debate, see Apel, Gadamer, et al., *Hermeneutik und Ideologiekritik* (Frankfurt am Main: Suhrkamp, 1971), and Paul Ricoeur, "Hermeneutics and the Critique of Ideology," in *Hermeneutics and the Human Science* (Cambridge: Cambridge Univ. Press, 1981), chap. 2.

The dispute, however, is itself broadening, and it now exposes different *modes* of interpretation occurring in human understanding.

2. For a more detailed analysis, see my "Interpreting Situations: An Inquiry into the Nature of Practical Theology," in *Formation and Reflection: The Promise of Practical Theology*, ed. Lewis Mudge and Daniel Poling (Philadelphia: Fortress Press, 1987).

3. For an excellent though more formal account, see Julian Hartt, "The Situation of the Believer," in *Faith and Ethics: The Theology of H. Richard Niebuhr*, ed. Paul Ramsey (New York: Harper & Row, 1957). In the present essay, I have expanded the meaning of Hartt's phrase to include the elements that come together in redemptive existence in the world.

4. That it is important for beliefs, attestations, and experiences to be "true," that is, to have to do with "reality," stems not only from the way faith occurs, and from the posture of the faithful person, but also from the human way of existing in situations as such. Faith's preoccupation with truth follows our general posture toward what Alfred Schutz calls the world of everyday life (*Collected Papers*, vol. 1, *The Problem of Social Reality* [The Hague: Martinus Nijhoff, 1967], 226). According to him, there is a "paramount reality" that human beings take for granted, a set of matters pertaining to survival itself.

5. Ecclesia, gospel, and faith are closely correlated with the threefold structure of theology or theological reflection, in which there is reference to a received content (tradition), the concern for truth, and the posture of action. There seems to be some convergence of recent theological opinion about theology's threefold structure; see my *Ecclesial Man* (Philadelphia: Fortress Press, 1975); David Tracy's *The Analogical Imagination* (New York: Crossroad, 1981), chap. 2; Charles Wood's *Discernment and Imagination: An Orientation in Theological Study* (Decatur, Ga.: Scholar's Press, 1985); and Dietrich Ritschl's *The Logic of Theology* (London: SCM Press, 1986).

6. James Gustafson is extremely alert to the multidimensionality of what he interprets. The two volumes of *Ethics from a Theocentric Perspective* (Chicago: Univ. of Chicago Press, 1981–84) repeatedly sort out and describe the elements of contexts both local and global. Thus, for instance, Gustafson affirms the "base points" of theological ethics to be "(*a*) the interpretation of God and God's relations to the world and particularly to human beings, and the interpretation of God's purposes; (*b*) the interpretation of the meaning or significance of human experience of the historical life of the human community, of events and circumstances in which persons and collectivities act, and of nature and man's participation in it; (*c*) the interpretation of persons and collectivities as moral agents, and of their acts; and (*d*) the interpretation of how persons and collectivities ought to make moral choices and ought to judge their own acts, those of others, and states of affairs in the world" (*Ethics* 2:143). Hence, Gustafson's own interpretation constantly exemplifies what I am calling a hermeneutic of situations. Nor is this synonymous in his work with his moral

analyses and constructive stands. But what he does not give us is a formal description of his hermeneutic method of situations. His own mode of interpretation is highly disciplined, but what goes into that disciplining is not thematized by him.

7. The theologian who in this century described redemptive existence by employing the category of response is well known: H. Richard Niebuhr. See his *The Responsible Self: An Essay in Christian Moral Philosophy* (New York: Harper & Row, 1963).

8. Hannah Arendt, *The Human Condition* (Chicago: Univ. of Chicago Press, 1958), 7; see also parts 2 and 4. In this essay I shall gloss over Arendt's distinction between labor and work and use the term "work" to designate primary occupation whether that occupation is oriented to perpetuating the conditions of life through bodily activity ("labor") or to producing transnatural artifacts ("work").

9. The sense of "vocation" as work interpreted in the framework of faith should be distinguished from two other familiar meanings. According to the first, vocation is the "calling" that originates faith itself (Rom. 8:28). According to the second, vocation is the divine call to a special (ordained) ministry and thus concerns the conditions and bases of priesthood and the ministry of the Word (cf. Acts 10:16).

10. With rare exceptions, the church, Catholic and Protestant, has not conceived its program of education for laity as ordered learning (see chap. 5 above). The teaching of religion in Catholic parochial schools may be an exception. But if church or congregational education does not have the character of ordered learning, it has little chance to discipline or rigorize fundamental modes of interpretation.

11. Specific schools have distinctive aims that are expressions of their special ways of responding to their contexts. A school of theological study will have its distinctive *environment* (ecclesiastical or secular, ecumenical or denominational, rural or urban), its *guiding idea* behind its general approach (piety or spirituality, scholarly rigor, pastoral skills), its vision of the nature and task of *church leadership* (sacramental, pastoral, interpretive, evangelistic), and reflecting all of that, its distinctive curricular *focus* (culture, doctrine, skills, praxis). The course of study of a specific school flows from all these things, and its academic *disciplines* and their organization inevitably reflect them. The disciplines of a school's faculty correlate with its curriculum, and its curriculum reflects its environment, guiding idea, focus, and theology of leadership.

12. This interpretation is elaborated in my *Theologia: The Fragmentation and Unity of Theological Education* (Philadelphia: Fortress Press, 1983), 84–94.

13. Although a careful analysis would require us to distinguish these, I use the terms referring to them more or less interchangeably in these chapters. When discussing the specific historical reality of Christianity as a content of university study, I speak of the "Christian religion." When discussing that

reality in clergy or church education, other terms are used, for instance, "Christian faith."

14. I do not think that interpreting the *subject matter* of theological study to be the Christian faith is necessarily a historicism or the abandonment of some other more apparently theological subject matter such as God, the Word of God, or salvation. It is seriously misleading to speak of God and the Word of God as subject matters of study. For that not only implies that these things are accessible to modes of study but that they are present to scrutiny in unmediated form. What we discover when we attempt to understand, explicate, or "study" any of these things is that to open them to study, we must make them thematic and determinate. The only way we can do this is through language and history. Even if we claim that revelation or grace forms the basis for our speaking of these things, when we *study* them we study them as manifest in a historic faith with its paradigmatic figure, originating events, classic texts, and the rest. What unifies the objects of religious study as objects of religious study is not God or the Word of God or salvation but the Christian faith.

15. Among matters of recent dispute in philosophy and theology is something called foundationalism. Criticisms of foundationalism reflect, as we would expect, the particular approaches of the schools doing the evaluating. Richard Rorty and neopragmatism, Heideggerian phenomenology, deconstructionism, and Anglo-American analytic philosophy all mount attacks on foundationalism. The target of the attacks is some remnant of the Platonic tradition that affirms the existence of metaphysical or epistemological grounds for human experience, knowledge, science, or philosophy itself. I hope that it is clear that what is under discussion in this chapter are foundations in a *pedagogical*, not epistemological, sense.

16. It is important to distinguish between studies that are foundational to other studies within a program of study and studies that are *propaedeutic* to the total program of study. A graduate program in psychology may require as foundational to its program a distinctive type of statistical studies, and these will occur in the program itself. On the other hand, the total graduate program may presume a certain level of education, certain minimal accomplishments in mathematics, and the like. These will determine the propaedeutic studies of the program. I make this distinction in order to say that this chapter is concerned with *foundational*, not *propaedeutic*, issues. I shall take up the matter of propaedeutic studies for theology in chap. 8.

17. Any suggestion that the disciplining of the mode of interpretation requires and builds on foundations will be suspected of perpetrating what Paulo Freire calls the banking model of education. In my view, a pure instance of the banking model in theological study is the theory-to-practice approach, which holds that objective learning provides information and skills for practice and application. But I do think that all the hermeneutic modes of the believer's situation require a specific and synthetic historical understanding of the Christian faith. This is the case even when we acknowledge that the historical

interpretation of the Christian faith is reciprocally facilitated and shaped by these modes. After all, through what and from what would the believer be interpreting the situation if the total determinate content of the Christian faith were bracketed? It could only be through and from the hegemony of a culture and social world. How can the truth and reality of faith and tradition even come into question given an utter ignorance of the historical content of the Christian faith? This natural presuppositional structure of foundations is distinguishable from a banking model in that the primacy of the Christian faith for the hermeneutic modes is not itself a specific and absolute pedagogical priority. In fact, the pedagogical requirements for understanding the dimensionality of the Christian faith in foundational studies may contravene the requirements imposed by the banking model.

18. Karl Rahner's outline divides the course of theological study into two parts: the *Grundkurs*, or basic level, and what occurs thereafter. Rahner calls one set of courses within the *Grundkurs* philosophy, and its theme is human being. It includes philosophical anthropology as well as explorations of human reality and is intended to afford the "transcendental" basis for the theology of God, salvation, and Christology (*Zur Reform des Theologiestudiums* [Freiburg: Herder & Herder, 1969]). In a similar vein, Francis Fiorenza proposes a course in "foundational theology" to introduce the hermeneutic experience of one's tradition which is at the heart of the study of theology. He means by this not the old apologetics or the foundations courses external to theology but rather studies in such themes as praxis, pluralism, and anthropology ("Foundational Theology and Theological Education," *Theological Education* 20 [1984]: 107–24). W. Pannenberg proposes anthropology, including theological anthropology, as a major aspect of theological studies (*Theology and the Philosophy of Science* [London: Darton, Longman & Todd, 1976]).

19. Although the primary focus of these chapters is on clergy education, it is important not to restrict the notion of foundational studies to the programs of studies of seminaries. The point is a broader one. Theological study has per se a structure that requires some things to be foundational, pedagogically, to other things. Consequently, some sort of foundational studies needs to be part of the theological study undertaken by the laity in churches and congregations. Some historical understanding of the themes of human being, culture, and Christian faith is presupposed by the hermeneutic modes whatever the environment or institution of study.

20. Any historical movement that continues into the present cannot be understood as simply a succession of periods with the present as its latest period. The current period is always that in which the older, even ancient, movement exercises a continuing influence: it is present as forgotten, marginal, transformed, legitimating, reinvigorated, splintered, and so forth. It is especially the case that modernity is not simply another period but an epoch that has effected and is effecting drastic change on all the movements surviving from earlier times. The movement of Christian faith is, therefore, not simply a

movement from its origins through patristic, medieval, and Reformation eras. It is a movement into the current epoch of modernity, and as a historical reality this faith cannot be identified with any one of its earlier forms, even that of its originating period. What it *is* includes how it functions in and is affected by modernity. The study of the Christian faith includes study of how it has fared in the modern world, its response to the communist movement, to the many phases of the Enlightenment tradition, to ecumenism, and to the sectarian splintering of Christendom. Thus, historical understanding of the Christian faith requires studies of nineteenth- and twentieth-century theology, and includes knowledge of the history of Christianity's relation to the sciences, its embodiment of Western patriarchalism, its reception of modern secularity, and its fate in both totalitarian and therapeutically oriented societies.

21. This requirement illustrates the interdependence of the modes of interpretation. The historical task of interpreting tradition and traditioning is assisted by interpretations of situations, action, and truth and reality. For this reason and in this sense, the person who is educated in historical interpretation must at the same time be educated in the hermeneutic modes that assist the study of the dimensionality and deep structures of historical reality.

22. Participation in a religious tradition in its character of bearing a claim, a reality attestation, about the sacred and about nature and the human world should not be thought of as a feature simply of Western religious faith. No believer is related to his or her religious and social world and mythos in utter cognitive indifference. The Bushmen of the Kalahari Desert of South Africa who see dreams as the deepest reality make a reality claim—one to be taken seriously by anyone who studies that religious faith.

23. The reduction of the pursuit of truth to data management is a recurring theme in Phillip Rieff's tracking of the emergent epoch and the cultureless society he calls therapeutic. For Rieff, an orientation toward truth is closely tied to a culture's ability to remember its traditioned past with the help of authorities that maintain societal interdicts. The "anything goes" of authorityless therapeutic society infects also the attitude to truth and transforms the question of truth into questions of style (*Fellow Teachers: Of Culture and Its Second Death* [Chicago: Univ. of Chicago Press, 1972], 196–97).

24. Some interpretations depict the High Middle Ages as opposed on principle to the progress of the sciences—and as having to self-destruct before modern science could be born. A more adequate account sees this period's relation to knowledge as ambivalent, and thus as not altogether unlike that of our own epoch's. The church, parodoxically, both spawned and persecuted challenges to its official cosmology. It settled whole areas of matter of fact by methods of authority, yet in articulating its faith drew on what it judged to be the most refined and advanced knowledge available to it. Virtually all doctrinal contents were explored in the light of not just the formal sciences—for instance, logic—but also psychology (philosophical anthropology), metaphysics, and natural philosophy. Thus, virtues and vices were so explained that their

human character was disclosed. God's providential activity was set forth with reference to the structure and movement of the world process. When we compare contemporary clergy education to this, we become acutely aware how much faith is today interpreted without any relation to the world's historical, human, and natural structures and processes. The unavoidable impression is that contemporary clergy education wants to understand God's world activity without relating it to the world and how the world proceeds through time. It wants to grasp sin as a corruption of power, society, and community without exploring what power, society, and community are. My objective is not to see faith displaced by "natural theology," which is a red herring of contemporary theology, but just to examine what is involved in faith's claims to truth and reality.

25. I use the term "action" rather than "praxis" self-consciously. Both terms have a long history, and the history, not to mention the variety in present usage, fosters equivocations. "Praxis" has the added burden of its politicization and its association with sloganizing rhetoric. As a term, "action" may carry fewer burdens. It is, besides, a term that connects us to the seminal works of Maurice Blondel and Hannah Arendt, as well as to action theory in the social sciences (Talcott Parsons) and the German and Anglo-American literature in the philosophy of action. I use the term more inclusively than Arendt, for whom it refers to the "only activity that goes on directly between men without the intermediacy of things or matter." For me, action coincides rather with Arendt's *vita activa* and thus includes labor and work in addition to action as she understands it.

26. The reason for this is pedagogical. Studied together, there is a better chance for these approaches to action to evoke and discipline a hermeneutic of action. They should be joined, however, in a *pedagogical*, not a *specialty*, area. If action became a topic limited to a coterie of specialists, its hermeneutic presence in other modes of interpretation would be lost and the responsibility of other areas to incorporate it would be undermined. Can we conceive of a historical interpretation of the Christian faith, or of struggles with truth and reality or with vocation, utterly without reference to action?

27. The comparative hermeneutics of world faiths has now become something of a self-conscious undertaking, with a growing literature. Wolfhart Pannenberg seems to have something like this in mind in his category of the science of religion, which includes both the theology and the history of religion (*Theology and the Philosophy of Science*, trans. Francis McDonagh [Philadelphia: Westminster Press, 1976], chap. 6, no. 2). One of the most explicit expressions of comparative hermeneutics is *The Cardinal Meaning: Essays in Comparative Hermeneutics*, ed. Michael Pye and Robert Morgan (The Hague: Mouton, 1973), where the focus is on a comparison of Buddhism and Christianity. See also W. C. Smith, *Toward a World Theology: Faith and the Comparative History of Religion* (Philadelphia: Westminster Press, 1981).

28. A significant literature marks both scholarly explorations of and actual

conversations between world faiths. There is a large literature of discussions between major world faiths: Christians with Muslims, Hindus, Buddhists, Jews; Muslims with Hindus, Christians, . . . See *Truth and Dialogue in World Religions*, ed. John Hick (Philadelphia: Westminster Press, 1974); H. J. Singh, *Inter-Religious Dialogue* (Bangladore, 1967); and *Christian Faith in a Religiously Pluralistic World*, ed. D. G. Dawe and J. B. Carman (Maryknoll, N.Y.: Orbis Books, 1978).

29. The School of Theology at Claremont has incorporated into its course of studies an annually changing focus on critical, global situations. A different selected theme pervades the life of the school and its curriculum each year.

30. The theme of work is not totally absent from the American pulpit and from the concern of the churches. But the way it is present reflects both the identification of vocation with the calling of the (ordained) leadership and the shape of a therapeutically oriented and technocratic society. The theme of work is broached in connection with the experience of work as stress. Needless to say, this does not approach work as a life situation posing issues of power, oppression, moral responsibility, and their like.

31. It goes without saying that the preparation for (ordained) church leadership requires a specific and distinctive program of study. Theological education in that specific sense was not what I was talking about when I used the phrase "the clerical paradigm" in *Theologia* (pp. 87–88) and "Practical Theology outside the Clerical Paradigm" (in *Practical Theology: The Emerging Field in Theology, Church, and World*, ed. Don Browning [San Francisco: Harper & Row, 1982], 26). The question at issue was the *nature of theology*. The clerical paradigm is a way of construing theology as strictly correlated to clergy education. Once theology itself is reduced to a phenomenon of clergy education, everything in clergy education is shaped by that reduction. I have criticized both the reduction and the shaping. For example, I argue that if theology is permitted to occur only in clergy education, "practical theology" will be narrowed to pastoral activity and training. There has been some unclarity on this point, according to Joseph Hough and John Cobb. They are not sure whether my arguments against the clerical paradigm repudiate the teleological element in clergy education. I intend no such repudiation, although I can see how I might be misunderstood. If clergy education is valid at all as a special instance of theological education, it will surely have its distinctive teleology. But theology itself cannot be defined by that teleology, and if clergy education is theological, it has a unity more complex than that in virtue of whatever distinguishes it as clergy education. I am not sure where Hough and Cobb stand on this point. They clearly accept the notion that theological education is education of all Christians, and this implies that the aims of clergy education cannot be the teleological element of all theological education. Yet, I am puzzled by one of their remarks: "Although we agree with Farley as to the importance of *theologia* as the basis for unity of theological education, we do not see that as minimizing the need for a 'teleological' unity. As Schleiermacher

saw, that unity is constituted by the aim to help educate professional leaders for the church" (*Christian Identity and Theological Education* [Chico, Calif.: Scholar's Press, 1985], 4). The contention seems to be that the unity of theological education as teleological is established by the aims of professional or church-leadership education. And this contradicts the acknowledgment that theological education is also something needed by all Christians which should occur in congregations.

8

The Structure of Theological Study: Disciplines and Curricula

I have distinguished between the structure of theological study and the curricula of specific educational programs. Structure, here, means the areas of study that theology, if taught, requires, and the relation between those areas. My thesis is that the *aim* of theological study is to discipline, or rigorize, the basic modes of interpretation that already exist in the situation of faith, and that these hermeneutic modes generate the requisites and criteria for the areas of study and the movement of study in the field. In the present chapter, I shall pursue four problems that arise when my thesis is brought to bear on actual programs of education. I shall discuss (*a*) the relation of the structure of theological study to scholarship and curricula; (*b*) the nature of theological study in congregational education and clergy education; (*c*) the relation between theological study and religious studies; and (*d*) the nature of the propaedeutic studies necessary to the study of theology.

Theological Study and Learning

The thesis of these pages may seem to come at a high price. Does the refusal to identify the structure of theological study with an organization of theological sciences end in anti-intellectualism? Does the claim that the hermeneutic modes constitute that structure make the sciences and scholarship irrelevant to theology? The case argued here may be construed as locating theology in the reflective life of the believer and thus as dislocating it from the schools, disciplines, and sciences. It may look as if an opposition is posited between theology and learning. I must try to head off such a disastrous misconstrual, which could empty theology of the critical principle altogether.

In chapter 5, I have made a case against restricting learning to clergy education and permitting "education" in only some lesser sense to congregations. Contending for an ordered learning for the believer as such, I oppose any opposition between theology and learning. Driving my argument is the premise that the believer's faithful life in situations needs not just the kind of interpretation that arises because human responses are as such interpretive but needs disciplined, self-aware interpretation. Such interpretation does not occur automatically but occurs instead through the disciplining and educational processes offered by a community. Ordered learning is appropriate to and needed by believers as such. Believers need not just "theology" but theological study—theology in the process of being shaped and disciplined by ordered learning. And that means theology as it occurs in a program of study and, thus, in the situation of teaching, with all its constitutive elements: teachers, cumulative knowledge, cognitive criteria, and a curriculum with its movement over time. The setting is *study*, and an environment of pedagogy. What happens when we introduce the structure of the hermeneutic modes into a program of study? The structure manifests itself in the *curriculum*, is pursued with the assistance of *scholarship*, and therefore engenders *disciplines*.

Why is it that the disciplining of interpretation needs and appropriates scholarship and the sciences? The most general reason is the intrinsic commitment of redemptive existence to the truth principle, to grasping and expressing the "way things are." Given a commitment to this principle, there is no way the advancing horizon of inquiry can be stopped. What is more, each hermeneutic mode occurs on an ever-moving horizon of inquiry that commandeers whatever cognitive resources are appropriate—from archaeology and linguistics to psychology and ontology. Nor does the allegiance to open-ended inquiry originate with post-Enlightenment modernity. Once faith acknowledges the validity and importance of understanding as such, it cannot say, "Thus far and no farther." The interrogation of reality can have no terminating point set in advance either for the religious community as a whole or for the individual believer. When the church sets forth its attestation and claim or when it engages in critical self-interpretation and educates its leadership and its constituency, it can have no grounds for curtailing its concern for the truth about things—even about the things of faith. The disciplining of reflective interpretation must go as far as the capabilities of human finitude permit. It must appropriate all available research, scholarship, sciences, and perspectival emphases. The result is that the disciplining of reflective interpretation must exist in an environment whose aims are centered in science and scholarship—in clergy schools, universities, and graduate schools.

How can the structure of theological study be embodied in a curriculum with disciplinary underpinnings? First, if each basic part of the structure of theological study is a mode of interpretation, the way these parts appear in ordered learning is as areas of hermeneutic. Insofar as schools or programs of study teach theology, they are teaching modes of interpretation. In short, theological study is, in the broad sense of the word, hermeneutic study. It is learning what is involved in the interpretation of tradition, action, truth, and work as they come together in situations. A pedagogical area (e.g., biblical studies) may bring together several disciplines—distinguishable pedagogical, scholarly undertakings—yet may be unified by the aim to thematize and rigorize one of the modes of interpretation (in this case, the hermeneutic of tradition in its originating events and texts).

Second, each of the hermeneutics requires knowledge of the area of concern and makes use of whatever sciences and scholarly resources are necessary for the disciplining of that mode of interpretation. We are familiar with the many humanistic and social sciences that are called on in the interpretation of early Christianity: polity, the philosophy of language, archaeology, history, classics. And in the interpretation of responsible action: sociology, political science, the history of philosophy, analytic or phenomenological methods. The relation between disciplines and the sciences is a pragmatic one: a discipline's pedagogical aim, along with its subject matter, prompts its selection of cognitive resources and methods.

We can see why thinking of the structure of theological study as a pattern for collecting sciences has had an unfortunate, even antiscientific, effect on the schools. By thinking of itself as a discrete science, a guild-supported discipline will immure itself in that science and thus lose the possibility of appropriating what it needs as a hermeneutic, as a disciplining of a mode of interpretation. Thus, we find pastoral psychology annexing psychology as its science and consequently feeling itself relieved of the obligation to read philosophical anthropology and the great "psychologists" of Western Christianity such as Augustine and Kierkegaard. We find ethicists reading the ethics literature and perhaps the auxiliary literature the graduate school encourages or permits but not the history of philosophy and theology, and not pastoral psychology. It is not that scholars within the disciplines must be totally eclectic and read everything. But the boundaries created for them by their self-understanding as scientists prevent them from crossing the boundaries even when their hermeneutic aims call for it. The pragmatic appropriation of needed scholarly resources is prevented by the guild-drawn boundary. When the disciplines or pedagogical areas think of themselves as sciences, they educate their students by furthering their guild sciences rather than by creating and refining distinctive hermeneutics: the systematic theologian does not teach theological thinking but passes on the texts, lingo, and issues of the guild; the homiletician by marrying biblical exegesis and rhetoric thinks to have gained release from the need to raise the question of the truth of the exegetically exposed material.

Third, the very subject matter, the Christian faith, properly delineates disciplines. In thinking about the Christian faith scholars have traditionally adopted an epochal approach, in which the faith is studied in major and minor periods and in its geographical and cultural distribution. Although there is nothing intrinsically wrong with epochal scholarship, it is not an adequate basis for organizing study of this subject matter, because epochs and regions do not trace the dimensionality of this historical reality. When religion is taught or studied in epochal specialties (New Testament literature, patristics, medieval Catholicism, the Reformation, European pietism, post-Enlightenment Christianity, American Methodism), the problem of understanding the religion is seen as the descriptive one of grasping the sequential movement of events, the contents of literatures, and the origins of movements. But all these together do not touch the religious faith in its claims about truth and reality, as a mythos for action, or as an institution of power, oppression, and traditioning. A more adequate approach organizes the disciplines along lines that yield an understanding of the *dimensions* of the historical Christian faith.

Finally, my interpretation of the nature of theological study calls for new curricular emphases, which in some cases will entail new scholarly disciplines. One new cognitive and pedagogical undertaking that I propose is the hermeneutic description of situations as such. If teaching in this area were developed, it would add a dimension to and perhaps redefine practical theology.[1] In this book "practical theology" is a comprehensive term, broadened to include three of the five hermeneutic modes: the hermeneutic of action, the hermeneutic of situations, and vocational hermeneutics.

I would give a more central place in theological study to two kinds of studies—perhaps disciplines—that have had a role in earlier periods: studies of world religions, and philosophy. Perhaps for reasons rooted in classical Protestant polemics against scholastic "natural theology" as well as in the classical Protestant principle of *sola scriptura*, philosophy has had only a marginal place in Protestant theological study. It has become relatively marginal in recent Catholic clergy education as well. This is a serious lapse not because we need to rehabilitate natural theology but because philosophy is the primary means of exposing, assessing, and making thematic the various paradigms of knowledge and reality that are subliminally or explicitly present in the responses of the church and the believer. Whether present in naive or examined forms, these paradigms dispose faith's interpretation of its own world and reality and of the larger culture. Furthermore, philosophy, which was virtually synonymous with the total human cognitive undertaking until the rise of modern science, has provided the conceptual framework for most of the major Christian theological visions from Christian Neoplatonism to process theology. Most important of all, philosophy, and not just the natural and social sciences, offers linguistic and phenomenological methods for studying the human being in its ontological structure, about which faith makes claims whenever it speaks of the realities of evil or the operations of grace.[2]

Theological Study and the Churches

Theology and theological study originate in the religious community, since "theology" in its primary sense designates the critical, reflective activity of the believer, and "theological study" the disciplining of that activity. It follows that the structure of theological study will be embodied in both lay, that is, congregational, and professional educational programs.

I have argued that church education should be theological education in the full and rigorous sense of ordered learning. The environment of church lay education is very different, however, from that of the university and the seminary. For one thing, the level of acculturation and formal education in the churches ranges from virtual illiteracy to the attainments of scientists and professionals. Illiteracy must be taken seriously by the church, since it is systemically connected to societal stratifications created by oppression and social disenfranchisement. Nevertheless, my comments will assume that the constituencies of the majority of North American congregations have a significant amount of public education. A second feature of the church environment springs from the fact that people participate in the church community over a long period of time. In a great many cases, life in the church begins with childhood and continues into adult maturity. So although a church cannot in its educative efforts build on a relative homogeneity of educational background, it can frame long-term educational programs that move from very introductory levels, suited to the education of children, to very advanced levels. The absence of a homogeneous educational background is not an absolute obstacle to ordered learning, learning that is rigorizing, sequential, and cognitively critical.

Ordered learning, however, varies with the environment in which it occurs. Schools of graduate and, some would say, "higher" education pursue it in conjunction with ongoing scholarly and scientific inquiry. Programs of church education would ordinarily seek a rigor of communication but not of research. Although all learning chases a moving horizon, the horizon of church lay education pertains to the reflective life and understanding of the believer and the community of faith, not the advance of scholarly investigation.

Since theological study is appropriate for the lay believer, the church's ordered learning, or education, should embody the structure and movement of theological study that we have already addressed. Church education, like all theological education, will be a rigorization of the basic hermeneutic modes: of tradition, action, situations, truth, and vocation. After all, the life of the lay person no less than that of the professional clergy is constituted by situations calling for response, interpretation, and understanding. The lay person also interprets situations under the guidance of tradition, responsible to the imperative of truth, serving a primary occupation, and oriented toward action. The very structure of theological study is born of the basic modes of interpretation operating in the believer's situation. It is odd, then, that there are notions of church education that pay no attention to the disciplining of those modes—which tack a Clergy Only sign on the hall of theological study. The idea of vocation that figures in church education is, of course, not that of the vocation of the ordained leadership. In the church the hermeneutic mode of vocation takes the form of interpreting both work—the primary occupation—and special ecclesial responsibilities. Church education can therefore legitimately include an ordered learning for teachers in the congregation. Nor can church education as theological education avoid rigorous study of theology's subject matter, the Christian faith. Nor can that study be reduced to "Bible study." Christianity's historical movement from its beginnings to the present, and in all its dimensions, must be the concern of church education.

Clergy education is a special instance of theological education, because its aim is to prepare a certain kind of church leadership. Schools and programs ordered by this aim need not exclude lay persons whose educational background and objectives require postbaccalaureate theological study. It is possible to envision a time when these schools will not be simply schools for clergy education. Their aims, however, will still cluster around the education of an advanced church leadership. Clergy education, which is in most but not all cases a postbaccalaureate program of studies, pursues theological study and ordered learning in the setting of ongoing scholarly work. It differs from church lay education and from university religious studies in two major respects. First, it teaches the basic modes of interpretation in such a way as to prepare church leaders themselves to teach, explore, and facilitate life in the church. Second, the total educational program is unified by the anticipated function of the student as a church leader: the focus of clergy education is vocation as a special, ecclesial work. Because of clergy education's vocational focus, ecclesiology should be a part of its foundational or initiating studies. What is disastrous is the idea that clergy education is simply professional training focused on ministerial skills, for that idea allows the distinctive professional aspect of clergy education to displace rather than to shape and supplement, and to be shaped and supplemented by, the structure of theological study. Clergy education, like congregational education, must find its own way of embodying the structure, the basic requirements, set by theology for theological study.

It is apparent that a hermeneutic approach to theological study requires rethinking the educational programs of clergy education. An adequate understanding of the Christian faith in its historical movement and dimensionality, and an adequate disciplining of the hermeneutic modes, pose a complex pedagogical challenge for clergy schools. To use a distinction from medieval Catholic education, present-day clergy education is only a "minor course," a series of beginnings, compared with the "major course" that historical and hermeneutic studies would require. The historical background and originating events of Christian faith cannot be grasped through introductory surveys of biblical literature and courses in exegesis; these courses are part of a pattern reflecting precritical ways of thinking. A vision of the formation, development, and fate of Christianity as a mythos, ethic, or doctrine does not accrete from one or two surveys of church history. An introductory course in ethics or a survey of the literature of liberation theology is only a modest beginning in the shaping of a self-conscious and disciplined hermeneutic of action. A postbaccalaureate three-year menu of introductory and survey courses, eked out with courses that focus the interests of several specialty fields, is not sufficient to the needs of the leadership of a religious faith desperately imperiled in the contemporary world. Theological study as advanced hermeneutic education requires a new institutionality of clergy education. If clergy education continues in its present institutional form—the three-year program of seminary studies, with roots in the early nineteenth century—the church needs to devise also a "major course" directed to a special type of church leader.

Theological Study and the University

In chapter 3, I built a case for giving theological studies a place in secular universities—in other words, for making them part of university programs in religious studies. But my analysis of the structure of theological study appears to be on a collision course with the case I built. The secular university, private or state-sponsored, has no responsibility for the well-being of specific religions or for serving their institutions and their educational needs. No one expects the local state university to train Jewish rabbis, Catholic priests, or Protestant ministers, nor to sponsor lay theological education for this or that denomination.[3] Yet I have contended that the primary meaning of theology is a wisdom and reflective activity that attend faith, and that faith occurs only through the historical mediation of the specific traditioning of a religious community. How, then, can theological study exist outside that community and its educational institutions? The nonreligious aims of the university seem utterly incompatible with the aims of theological study. To put the problem slightly differently, my view of the conditions, context, and aim of theological study appears to be *fideist,* limiting such study in principle to faith communities, and this fideism seems to undercut any case for theological study in the university.

The apparent contradiction presents us with the question of what is involved in the study—in the understanding, interpretation, scholarly investigation, historical knowledge, critical appraisal—of a specific religious faith. I assume that there is nothing about the study of religion and of specific religions that is incompatible with the scientific and pedagogical aims of the university. I also assume that specific religions are not so mysterious and esoteric that they cannot be studied at all. In other words, I assume that specific religions allow themselves to be understood through a variety of methods, that they are, in short, available to understanding and interpretation.

What is available? Clearly, the history, social reality, and practices of a religious faith can be studied. Early Buddhism, present-day Eastern European Judaism, and Plains Indian religion are all accessible to historical, linguistic, archaeological, and other modes of inquiry. But clearly too, we have not understood Judaism, have not even studied it as itself, if we do not understand it as a *faith.* Nor will Judaism, Christianity, and other religious faiths be understood *as faiths* without grasping the way these faiths are multidimensional realities. Moreover, each faith is multidimensional in a distinctive way that requires its own basic modes of interpretation. If this is the case, any thoroughgoing study of religion will face the tasks set by theological study: the understanding and interpretation of a subject matter (Jewish, Christian, Buddhist faith), and the grasp of basic modes of interpretation. The *interpretation* of a religious faith requires entering into the *interpretations,* that is, the hermeneutic modes, constituting that faith.

There is a difference between theological study that occurs within and on behalf of a community of faith and the more distanced study of that community's faith. Within a faith, the aim of study is the disciplining of faith's actual reflective life; this occurs in the institutions and among the constituents of the religious faith. In the more distanced study of a faith, the aim of theological study is to understand the religious faith; this requires entering into specific hermeneutic modes to the degree that that advances the understanding. The difference, however, should not be thought of as between a personally, existentially oriented and an impersonally, objectively oriented study. If it were thought of in that way, theological study within a faith would be permitted interest in questions of the truth of the interpretations studied and of the wisdom of the presented imagery, whereas "objective" scholarly studies of a faith would be expected to proceed in a posture of indifference to such things. This posture of nonjudgmental neutrality pervades much of present-day humanistic and social-scientific pedagogy, but it is corruptive of the university. The deepest reason for the study of anything is to discipline the modes of interpretation—political, aesthetic, scientific, social, personal, or whatever. One studies ancient Buddhism for the same reason one studies Freud, James Joyce, or Whitehead. Something is being laid claim to in these texts which may have to do with reality and truth, with the way things are, could be, or should be. Utter existential indifference to the truths posed by or laid claim to in the subject matter is a deadly virus, a virtual AIDS of education, any education. Although the educational aims of religious and nonreligious institutions are different, both kinds of institution must include studies that seek to understand and to be shaped by whatever wisdom and truth can establish itself, however historically specific its origin and context.

All religious faiths are socially and historically determinate. Believers in whatever faith exist in situations and respond to and interpret the mystery of things on the basis of the mediations of tradition. Grasping the stars as great hunters is a way of construing things for the African Bushmen, and as such it is an interpretation. Understanding any religious faith requires entrance into the circle of its own self-understanding, into the matters it is serious about, the claims embodied in its tradition-formed experience. The study of any religion therefore entails and requires a study of the dimensions of that religion's faith and of the correlative types of interpretation. The basic hermeneutic modes of that religion must be studied. In reflective interpretation requiring rigorization, the Christian faith comes to self-conscious understanding. To study the religious faith seriously is to be pressed by the claim it sets. But anyone who wishes to grasp the religion at the level of its own claim and self-understanding, in other words, as a *faith*, must appreciate the structure of its reflective interpretations—of its theology. This is why the student must enter into the modes of interpretation that structure the religion's world of faith, and into the study of theology.

If a program of religious studies includes the study of the Christian religion and construes that study to be only a study of classical materials from the faith's origins (Old Testament, New Testament), it has bought into a very truncated vision of its own potential. The teaching and understanding of Christianity will be narrow and abstract if the university student ignores the religion in its truth claims and if no attention is paid to the way its mythos shapes human action or to the distinctive way its believers are prompted to exist interpretively in situations. Thus, the study of a specific religion must attempt to enter into that religion's own hermeneutic structure, in other words, the structure of theological study. Nor is there anything about the effort which is in conflict with the university's critical temper or its commitment to scholarship. On the contrary, to rule out the study of a religious faith's structure of self-interpretation is surely arbitrary and a contravention of the university's cognitive and pedagogical aims.

Each religious faith has distinctive elemental dimensions and distinctive basic hermeneutic modes. Hence, the structure of Christian theological study will not be identical to that of Jewish or Buddhist theological study. There will also be differences between how the study of theology occurs in the Christian church's educational institutions and how it occurs in the secular university. The truth orientation of the religious community toward the realities to which it attests creates a basic posture in its educational undertakings. In the university, the primary agenda of inquiry concerns religious faiths as *historical* phenomena. Given that agenda and posture, the way the structure of theological study might appear in religious studies in the university reflects the dimensions of a religious faith as a *historical* reality. Religious faiths as comprehensive historical entities offer themselves to study in three dimensions: the historical, the social, and the symbolic-linguistic. Given this, does the Christian faith set requirements on the inquiry and pedagogy of those who would teach it in the university?

Whatever else it is, the Christian faith is an enduring *historical* reality. To the extent that its history is retrievable, it properly evokes historical specialties that focus on origins and epochs of development. Because history is itself multidimensional, these specialties properly reflect a variety of historiographies. The focus, however, must be on the faith as a historical entity and, therefore, on all the matters that make up a historical entity.

Some scholars may think of the *social* study of Christian faith as a special type of historiography. But the sociality of a religion is a particular dimension of its reality and calls for a distinctive approach and conceptual framework. As a social reality, a religious faith is a distinct form of human intersubjectivity. It creates distinctive institutions and distinctive social ways of enduring through time. Furthermore, it is constituted by distinctive social structures of leadership, ritual enactment, and corporate constituency. It occurs in the context of the larger society and stands to society in relationships of opposition, sanction, isolation, and so forth. It can legitimate the oppressive elements of the larger society, oppose them, or paradoxically, do both. The sociality of religion is, in short, a dimension sufficiently complex and important to justify a discrete research agenda, a discipline. To make the investigation of the sociality of religion one of the tasks of some other compartment of labor in the university is probably to bury it.

The Christian faith, like all religious faiths, is also a mythos, a symbolic-linguistic account of reality that brings together themes of the human condition and the sacred. The characteristic language of the mythos, written or oral, is narrational. The primary symbols, narrations, and dogmas of the faith's mythos combine a doxological orientation with an orientation to truth and reality. To grasp the mythos of the faith draws on, but also goes beyond, historical and social inquiries.

Each of these three dimensions of historical Christianity calls forth appropriate resources of scholarship. History requires knowledge and specialty tools pertinent to the epoch. For instance, the study of ancient Hebrew religion will draw on archaeology, on Hebrew and the other languages of the ancient Near East, and on ancient Near Eastern history, as well as on tools dictated by the historiographical emphasis— intellectual history, institutional history, or whatever. The social study of historical Christian faith draws on the sociology of religion, in the sense of a data-oriented social scientific methodology, but it must draw on much more than this. It must call into service social philosophy, social psychology, *Ideologiekritik,* the "genealogical" methods of Michel Foucault, and the social-world analysis of Alfred Schutz. The symbolic-linguistic study of Christianity must draw on more than simply the philosophy of religion, especially in its narrower sense of rational theology. It must also appropriate the philosophy of language, philosophical anthropology, and the hermeneutics of symbols and myths.

These three dimensions of historical Christianity—the historical, the social, and the symbolic-linguistic—can demarcate pedagogical areas and areas of scholarly study concerning the Christian religion in the university.[4] They also suggest a general pattern for the study of any specific faith, or even a way of organizing a general program of religious studies.

The Issue of Propaedeutic Studies

Education in the sense of ordered learning necessarily has a temporal movement. The ordering of learning is, at least partly, ordering in sequence, not only because it is impossible to learn everything at once but also because the understanding of some things presupposes the understanding of others. In the study of physics the student who knows no mathematics will not go very far. In theological study too, some things must be studied as a condition of understanding other things.[5] All theological study takes for granted and builds on prior stages of ordered learning. That all theological study requires studies prior to itself has been a conviction in the church since medieval times, when the universities required the trivium (grammar, logic, and rhetoric) and the quadrivium (arithmetic, geometry, astronomy, and music) as preparation for studying theology. The same conviction has helped shape the North American institution of clergy education, the theological—and usually, denominational—seminary, which almost always requires a liberal-arts education prior to admission. Despite the requirement, however, discussion of the idea behind the requirement is today languishing. There is little debate today over exactly which studies theological study requires as a precondition for its fruitful pursuit.[6]

It is not hard to fathom the reasons for this. Most schools of clergy education, pressed by the threat of low enrollment, always worried about finances, and in fierce competition with one another, admit over ninety percent of their applicants. In their extremity, not many schools can afford to have tough, or even clear, policies about preseminary educational preparation or to impose in situ remedial requirements. On top of this, their self-understanding as training or technical schools for a profession leads them to mimic the larger circle of professional schools, most of which regard the baccalaureate or its equivalent as enough for admission. Besides, when clergy education is a cluster of introductions to various clergy-related subject matters, it is not governed by aims that require an internal movement with a basis in preseminary education. If there is any internal movement, it is from theory to practice, and the liberal arts in general are all that are required for entrance to that minor procession. Too, the undergraduate degrees of present-day colleges and universities are so widely varied in their quality and content that most postbaccalaureate schools are defeated in advance of specifying propaedeutic studies for those they admit.

The question of what theological study requires is not, of course, one only for clergy education. If theological education is education, that is, ordered learning, it will require some educational background whatever its level and environment. Most generally, the question is what kinds of learning are needed in virtue of the subject matter, namely, the Christian faith, and in virtue of the nature of the hermeneutic modes. It is clear, for instance, that theological interpretation directed to the traditioned past is assisted by methods, skills, and knowledge that are broader than those found in the tradition itself. This is the case because the traditioned past comprises events, texts, persons, and historical change. Thus, propaedeutic to theological study is some acquaintance with the basic modes of interpretation as such.[7] The following analysis pertains to theological study as it occurs in a postbaccalaureate course of studies and hence describes propaedeutic studies as they would occur at the college level.

Theological study combines a subject matter, the Christian faith, with fundamental modes of interpretation. What preparation does the postbaccalaureate student need who would engage in those studies? Certain answers are obvious that have to do with the aims and contents now constituting liberal-arts education. Literacy, linguistic skills, and familiarity with history, sociology, and literature all form part of the groundwork for the study of the Christian religion as a complex historical reality. Current clergy education tends to assume that liberal-arts education in this sense is sufficient preparation for theological study. This assumption may be defensible insofar as theological study is simply a specialized form of general (humanistic, social-scientific) studies. If, however, the aim of theological study is to discipline certain basic modes of interpretation that represent a growing understanding of the Christian faith in its several dimensions, a general spread of liberal-arts studies is not sufficient. What more is needed than the liberal-arts curriculum?

It is difficult to answer this question apart from a critical analysis of the present state and meaning of the liberal arts. The liberal arts as they might be encountered in some ideal four-year course of post-high-school studies covering a wide range of disciplines could afford an adequate foundation for theological study. But today the disciplines and departments that serve up the liberal arts to undergraduates are likely to be aggregates of specialties, and as such they communicate specialty-oriented methods rather than comprehensive modes of interpretation. It is a contemporary tragedy that one can be a history major and yet never grasp the historical in its dimensional variety. Oriented by specialist research methods, the major can understand an era or event "historically," without any reference to traditioning, social continuity, the repression of language by sedimentations of power, or the deep structures of a mythos. The major can end up with little or no notion of what is involved in the interpretation of very difficult texts from Plato, Dante, and Darwin, since social- and text-hermeneutic matters are sloughed off as tasks for other specialties and other majors. In today's liberal arts the aggregate of sociology courses does not produce, except in the narrow sense of research methods, a general hermeneutic of social worlds, of deep social structures. The examples could go on and on, and they reach even to religious studies, where the courses rarely come together to give the student a sense of the hermeneutic complexity of religions—of their bid for ontological, theological, historical, and linguistic appraisals. Liberal-arts education is not what it could be: education so oriented to the dimensional complexity of reality that basic hermeneutic orientations are brought out. But it is precisely this which theological study requires as a dimensional study of the Christian faith and a disciplining of modes of interpretation.

What would the ideal program of studies propaedeutic to theological study embrace? First, the graduating senior would be vastly more prepared not only for theological study but for any graduate and professional study if the liberal arts could produce self-conscious, disciplined, and general hermeneutic orientations—historical, aesthetic, ontological, social, and linguistic, to mention a few. In addition, three sorts of propaedeutic studies lay an especially crucial groundwork for theological study: historical-cultural, philosophical, and religious studies.

Faith, we recall, is redemptive existence in the world, that is, in situations. The interpretive responses constitutive of faith read situations theologically. But if the interpretive responses are made in complete innocence of the major modes of interpretation that have arisen outside theology in recent centuries, they will tend toward biblicism, moralism, and precritical applications of authority. The theological reading of situations is not the same thing as a psychoanalytic, praxist, phenomenological, or technological reading. But in each of those readings, interpretation has become self-conscious, thematized, and rigorous. The interpretation has uncovered dimensions of historical and human reality that cannot be ignored without seriously distorting the theological reading of situations. Therefore, some acquaintance with the major seminal interpretive and hermeneutic orientations, Eastern and Western, is crucial as background for theological study that is itself hermeneutic in its aims.

Historical-cultural propaedeutic studies can acquaint the student with major movements of thought that have the character of world interpretations. But historical-cultural studies must also address our present situation of local and world cultures. Therefore, they should include studies in the "three worlds" (noncommunist, communist, and Third World), Eastern studies, and studies in minority and feminist history and in North American culture and its social and intellectual history. College degree programs offer at best only a cursory survey of such topics. The point, however, is that the student who anticipates postbaccalaureate theological study should know that cultural-historical studies are important bases for the hermeneutics of situations and action, as well as for the dimensional study of the Christian faith.

The second sort of propaedeutic studies, *philosophical* studies, will not be enthusiastically pursued by most current preseminary students.

The programs of study of the seminaries encourage this disinterest. North American Catholic clergy education has moved away from the two-stage, philosophy-to-theology approach. This, joined with the time-honored Protestant suspicion of philosophy, results in seminary programs in which philosophical study is very marginal if it is not totally ignored. Moreover, given the disputes about the nature of philosophy and even the politicizing of this pedagogical area in the university, not everything that goes by the name of philosophical studies in the university will have a propaedeutic potential for the study of theology. The philosophy that theological students need as background must be broad enough to include the current disputes as well as convey the rich historical legacy of philosophical attempts to reflect on the mystery of things. Some empiricist-analytical and Continental philosophies build the case for themselves by trying to discredit the philosophical past. Such approaches, which amount virtually to philosophical ideologies, may arrest rather than advance the development that the student seeks in preparing to study theology.

Philosophical studies are central, even necessary, to theological studies for several reasons. First, whatever the reigning school or approach, philosophy brings a legacy of classic texts that require a certain way of reading which is itself hermeneutic. To read Plato's *Republic* or Whitehead's *Modes of Thought* is to have to think with the author. Simply to follow the thought development of these texts is to think in a certain way. The majority of postbiblical and seminal Christian texts are similar to philosophical texts in this respect, and many of the Christian texts are written from, against, or in the framework of the classic philosophical texts. I am increasingly convinced that seminary students are intimidated by theological texts because they have never been prepared to think in the way required for understanding them.

Second, philosophy has to do with conceptual frameworks of interest to theology. The subject matter of theological study is the Christian faith in its dimensions, historical movement, and current situation. And the historical Christian faith has always appropriated, altered, or opposed the conceptual frameworks that have arisen outside theology. Until the rise of the sciences in the modern sense, "philosophy" was the name for the human effort to understand the world. To lack knowledge of philosophy in this sense is to miss the conceptual frameworks in which Christian theology was conceived and by which it has understood itself. It is also to miss knowing how the Christian movement was and continues to be subjected to criticism and how it fares under that criticism. The Christian faith's struggle with its own truth and reality occurs in dialogue with the culture's reigning reality paradigms. Theological study that is oblivious of this dialogue practices the hermeneutic of truth and reality only in a trivialized sense.

Third, philosophy is an ally of theology in the struggle against scientism. Philosophy struggles with the mystery of things not through the mythoi of specific historical faiths but in a wider, more general framework. Although this struggle is never utterly transcultural, philosophy aims at a kind of universality in its treatment of the themes of language, sociality, being, mind, and moral obligation. It is just philosophy's more general reflection that questions whether the valid but abstracted results of research in the sciences exhaust reality. Furthermore, philosophy sometimes turns its more general reflection toward the mysteries of knowledge, experience, reality, and the human being as such. If theology is to avoid a mere dualist and compartmentalized way of relating redemptive existence to the world of the sciences, it must take into account philosophy's more general reflection on the mystery of things. Compartmentalized theology lives in two separate worlds—the world of faith and the world of the sciences. It consequently has no basis for relating the realities of redemption to actual human beings in their flesh, sociality, and time consciousness. If theology wishes to understand how its claims about human being, the world, and history fit with the more general features of those things, recourse is necessary to a wider reflection on the mystery of things—in other words, to philosophy. Otherwise, theology will find itself confronting the world only through the abstracting grid of scientific research. The end result will be that it is relating its claims about human evil and redemption to data and not to human being, history, and nature.

A third set of studies propaedeutic to theology is *religious* studies. The field of religious studies is an especially important part of the preparation needed by the student who wants to study theology, since current clergy education, which is little more than a sequence of surveys and general introductions, does not offer the theological student sufficient studies in religion.[8] The name "religious studies" does not so much project a clear consensus about the study of religion as collect a mélange of studies ranging from courses of the kind found in the seminary (e.g., New Testament) to courses about Japanese Buddhism and about religion and literature. But religious studies is important for what knowledge it does offer of religion itself and the historic religions. The discussions and disputes over the nature of religion and the interrelations of religions are about something that the Christian faith is a part of. Furthermore, in courses in religious studies the student can learn something about Christianity's understanding of itself, whether as a (true) religion or, even, as something transcending the genre of religion.

Students can best profit from postbaccalaureate programs of theological study if their general liberal-arts studies are drawn together along the lines of basic interpretive modes, if they know something about the major modern hermeneutic movements, if they have emphasized historical-cultural studies that give some notion of the tangle in current situations, if they have pursued philosophical studies far enough to know some of the classic philosophical texts and to have thought along with the writers of the texts, and if they have made a start in religious studies.[9] Insofar as college programs fail the student, clergy education must give serious consideration to establishing its own remedial programs. This book offers more a vision of possibility than specific prescriptions for action. The vision is elusive, because the structure of theological study is a kind of ideality, a set of desiderata, that should preside over the teaching of theology whatever the environment of the teaching. At the heart of the vision is the perception that theology has to do both with the specific historical reality of the Christian faith and with the hermeneutic modes engendered by the situation of faith. I believe that the clouding of this perception goes far to explain why theological study is not faring well in the environments where it exists and why it has not entered other environments—for example, church education—where it should exist. I have not wished to understate the significance of the visions informing the two models of the structure of theology which my own model supplants—those of theological study as clergy education and as a pattern of sciences. But I would hope that both clergy education and theological scholarship would profit from increased clarity about what they depend on, namely, the basic hermeneutic modes operative in the situation of faith.

NOTES

1. For thoughts on the expansion of the meaning of practical theology, see the essays collected in *Practical Theology: The Emerging Field in Theology, Church, and World,* ed. Don Browning (San Francisco: Harper & Row, 1982), esp. those by David Tracy, Thomas Ogletree, and Dennis McCann.

2. Karl Rahner makes a strong case for including philosophy in theological study; his approach is different from what he calls the Roman approach, where only philosophy is the propaedeutic predecessor to theology (*Zur Reform des Theologiestudiums* [Freiburg: Herder & Herder, 1969], 40–41). Wolfhart Pannenberg makes a similar case, arguing that the claims of theology imply philosophical hypotheses about reality as a whole (*Theology and the Philosophy of Science,* trans. Francis McDonagh [Philadelphia: Westminster Press, 1976], chap. 5, nos. 3–4).

3. This statement is not completely confirmed in fact. A recent study, yet to be published, of theology and religious studies in the Southeast discovered many instances, some in state universities, where the teaching of religion was arranged in such a way that the cause of a particular religion—in this case, Christianity—was advanced. There were, e.g., cases where the introductory courses to religion were "Old and New Testament" courses. And some courses taught by state universities reflected the aims of clergy education or preclergy education. See Stan Lusby and Linda Tober, "Religious and Theological Studies in the Southeastern United States" (a preliminary report).

4. Under discussion here is how Christian studies might occur in the university. Insofar as any religion possesses these three dimensions, they can serve to organize the field of religious studies itself. The pedagogy fostered by such a division of labor would be oriented toward understanding religion in and through the hermeneutic modes. The unity of the field of religious studies would then lie in its study of religion and religions in their distinctive dimensionality and claims. This unity would make a strong case for considering religious studies a distinctive undertaking irreducible to the occasional undertakings of the study of religion within the various humanistic and social sciences of the university.

5. Insofar as there is movement in the theological curriculum of postbaccalaureate clergy education, there is a sort of ordered learning. Clergy education is thus a course of studies, and church education is not. There is a kind of movement in church education which follows the levels of communication demanded by human growth and development, but there is no real curricular movement that builds on earlier stages. Church education has no curriculum in the sense of a course of studies and ordered learning. There are exceptions to this in some individual congregations, especially in conservative denominations. For an elaboration of this point, see chap. 5 above.

6. Propaedeutic concerns are evident in postbaccalaureate clergy education in the catalogue statement of desiderata. This list of desired pretheological

studies articulates not requirements for admission, however, but rather suggestions for course planning.

7. I am thinking here of liberal-arts education—distinguished from career and research-specialty education—as *hermeneutic* education. I take its aims to be to evoke and discipline a variety of modes of interpretation: historical, linguistic, empirical, political, and aesthetic.

8. Postbaccalaureate clergy schools sometimes see liberal-arts religious and theological studies as unnecessary for the seminary-bound student. Yet, the more the three-year M.Div. course of studies takes on the character of a series of introductions to a variety of subjects, the less it is able to deepen the fundamental hermeneutic modes. In the seminary, students are acquainted with New Testament literatures, with a smattering of the history of Israelite religion and early Christianity, with part of the sweep of the history of Christianity, with doctrinal loci, and with the rudiments of pastoral care, preaching, and church administration. If there is a curricular movement in this collection of introductions, it is not toward the forming of an ever larger portrait of Christian faith or a deepening of interpretive modes but is just a journey from one introduction to another. Hence it is imperative that religious and theological studies begin before and continue after the M.Div. course of studies, as that is conceived at present.

9. If theological study can take place in church lay and university undergraduate education, we cannot avoid asking what is propaedeutic to theological study in those settings. In my judgment, background studies are required similar to those for clergy education. If theological study works toward an ever growing portrait of Christian faith, then whatever is necessary or helpful to that objective needs to be part of the preliminary course of study. This seems to be as true for church lay education as for clergy education. Nevertheless, since church education does not see itself as a course of studies, such a notion will seem very foreign—virtually an impossibility. Philosophical and religious studies will likewise seem alien intrusions upon church education. This, however, may be more the result of a longstanding way of thinking than a pedagogical impossibility. Once church education is thought of as a lifelong course of studies beginning in childhood and more or less making use of public education's results, there is no reason that historical-cultural, philosophical, and religious studies cannot occur in the ordered learning of the church at appropriate levels of teaching.

Index